Lutz Libert
Tobacco, Snuff-Boxes and Pipes

Lutz Libert

Tobacco, Snuff-Boxes and Pipes

Orbis · London

Translated from the German by Sheila Marnie

Design: Walter Schiller

© 1984 by Edition Leipzig
First published in Great Britain by Orbis Publishing Limited, London 1986.

Printed in the German Democratic Republic
ISBN 0-85613-918-1

Introduction

From the very earliest times writers have mentioned the inhalation of narcotic plant vapours for medical and ritual purposes. Herodotus (c. 484–425 B.C.) describes how the Scythians used the narcotic smoke of hemp. The Roman scholar, Pliny the Elder, who died in the eruption of Vesuvius in 79 A.D., reported in his *Natural History* on the curative effects which the smoke produced from burning the flowers and leaves of coltsfoot (*Tussilago farfara*) had on persistent coughs. Plutarch (c. 46–120 A.D.) mentions the Teutons using a kind of grass (he does not identify it more precisely), the tips of which they threw on the fire. The resulting smoke was inhaled and a narcotic stupor thereby induced.

"Elves" pipes, "fairy pipes" or "Celtic pipes" are the popular names given to the many discoveries of iron, bronze or clay pipes made among the remains of Roman military camps. It is probable that pipes made of such materials were widely used by Roman auxiliaries.

No precise scientific examination of these finds has been made, but in some cases the pipes have proved to be either of more recent origin or to be actual fakes.

It was only after the discovery of the American continent that the tobacco plant reached Europe and its use became widespread. When Christopher Columbus made his first American landfall in the West Indies, he and his comrades were the first Europeans to witness tobacco-smoking natives. Las Casas, an early historian of the Conquest, mentions the way Indians carried around herbs wrapped in a dried leaf, and that they would light one end and suck in the smoke from the other end. These bundles the Indians called *tabacos*.

In 1502, during his exploration of Florida, Juan Ponce de León noticed Indians smoking tobacco in clay pipes. Other contemporary reports speak of the use of snuff and the chewing of a mixture of tobacco and chalk in Central America. Many Indian tribes had myths and legends which spoke of the reverence accorded to the tobacco plant and the tobacco pipe. In addition to using tobacco for curative purposes and ceremonial rituals it was already common for it to be used purely for pleasure.

In 1579 Anton Schneeberger, personal physician to King Stephen Bathory of Poland (1576–1586), described the new fashion of smoking in Europe: "Almost all the sailors who return from the West Indies have the habit of putting little funnels of palm leaves or straw filled with rolled dried tobacco leaves in their mouths. They then light these and inhale as much of the smoke as they can. They claim that this helps combat hunger and thirst, gives strength and a feeling of happiness. They also maintain that the smoke calms the brain with a pleasant inebriation by filling the passages of the brain with aromatic vapours."

Pharmacists and doctors were the first to turn their full attention to the tobacco plant and cultivate it in Europe. In 1560 the French ambassador Jean Nicot brought the first plants to France from Portugal, where they were growing as botanical curiosities in the palace gardens. From there the plant spread across Europe with a speed unmatched by any other overseas product. By 1600 *herba nicotina*—the scientific name given to tobacco by the botanist Delachamp—was known in all the countries of Europe. In 1565 Dr. Adolf Occo, municipal physician in Augsburg, received the seeds for the first cultivation of the plant in Germany. In

1

6 Hungary, cultivation started in 1568, followed by Italy in 1579.

In addition to being a decorative plant, tobacco was now gaining increasing importance as a medicinal cure-all. Tobacco juice was prescribed for the "French disease", leaves were laid on wounds to heal them or used to remove sores or relieve unlocalized headaches. Tobacco enemas were used for constipation. As late as 1812 British military doctors still carried in their bags apparatus for the application of tobacco smoke in the case of soldiers rescued from drowning. Only when Posselt and Reimann isolated the main alkaloid, nicotine, in 1828, was it possible to prove scientifically how harmful tobacco was.

Tobacco used as snuff represented a transitional form between medicinal use and use for pleasure. Originally it was used to cure headaches and eye-ache, but within a few decades it became a fashionable pastime with its own ritual and ceremony.

It was colonists returning from an unsuccessful attempt to settle in Virginia who brought tobacco and clay pipes fashioned in the Indian style back to England. Sir Walter Raleigh (1554–1618) was responsible for making clay pipes socially acceptable. In England the independent production of clay pipes developed around 1600. Sailors, soldiers and students spread the habit of smoking throughout Europe. Central Europe was introduced to pipe-smoking mainly by the large numbers of armies which crossed and recrossed Europe during the Thirty Years' War (1618–1648). Hans Jakob C. von Grimmelshausen, in his novel *Simplicius Simplicissimus*, complained that "nine out of ten people indulge in various forms of tobacco".

Another form of smoking reached Europe via Spain: the cigar. The Mexican Aztecs and the inhabitants of the West Indies used to smoke rolled-up tobacco leaves. The Mayas put these rolled-up leaves into highly decorative and valuable pipes to smoke them.

The cigarette with its paper sheath is almost as old as the pipe or the cigar. In 1575 a Spanish doctor reported from Mexico to the court in Madrid that the natives produced paper which they used to put round rolled tobacco.

The nicotine in tobacco can enter the human body in a variety of ways. Snuff-takers, pipe- and cigar-smokers take it into their blood through the mucous membranes of the nose and throat. Cigarette-smokers inhale most of the smoke and it enters the bloodstream via the lungs. Cigar and pipe tobacco are basic tobac-

DE TABAKS PLANT.

1 The tobacco plant, surrounded by products derived from its leaves. From: Feinhals, J., Der Tabak in Kunst und Kultur. *Cologne 1926*

cos largely free from soluble carbohydrates. In the case of cigarette tobacco a high sugar content is necessary if it is to be properly enjoyed. Nicotine is combined here with acids, and during combustion acid components form which neutralize existing bases. A cigarette-smoker therefore derives little pleasure from other forms of tobacco, and vice-versa.

There is convincing medical evidence that deep inhalation of cigarette smoke is a decisive causal factor in many bronchial, cardiac and circulatory complaints. The UN health organization and many national medical bodies have introduced vigorous campaigns to reduce the damage to health caused by smoking. Basically, tobacco is similar to other products which are bought and used for the purposes of pleasure, and is open to abuse whatever method is used to take it—smoking, sniffing or chewing.

In times of war, or in the hard times in the aftermath of war, tobacco consumption increased sharply. Soldiers received tobacco rations as a stimulant against hunger and fatigue. Women used cigarettes to give them momentary relief from exhaustion. Tobacco was easy to use, could be taken almost anywhere and its pleasant effects were immediate, so it quickly became popular.

This book looks at the paraphernalia of tobacco-smoking—tobacco tins, snuff-boxes, pipes, cigar- and cigarette-holders. These objects have been subject to the styles and fashions of the times in which they were produced and used. But, inversely also, tobacco-smoking has had an influence on fashions in clothing, and on certain social forms and customs in many countries. The abundance of information makes it necessary to confine this investigation to the countries of Europe. It is not arranged according to periods in the history of art, but rather according to the various objects themselves.

After a description of snuff-boxes we look at the most common group of objects—pipes. The use of cigars, cigarettes and chewing-tobacco only has a limited number of objects associated with it and the section on these is therefore relatively brief.

Concentration merely on "antique" *objets d'art* has been deliberately avoided. Instead an attempt has been made to demonstrate that certain traditions have been retained over the centuries or have continued in a more modern form.

The material and aesthetic value of many objects associated with smoking has meant that from early times these have been sought-after by collectors. The first collections of snuff-boxes and pipes were made by absolutist rulers. Then the bourgeoisie, and also tobacco firms themselves, started to collect objects connected with the history of tobacco. The motive now was less that of owning exclusive objects of value but more a genuine interest in preserving the historical heritage, and also simply the pleasure to be derived from such charming miniatures.

This book is intended to serve as an aid to collectors and admirers of such objects.

The illustrations originate from many museums and collections throughout Europe, but mainly from Central Europe. In particular in the case of sectioned pipes it is clear that forms have developed in this part of Europe which have few equivalents in other countries and certainly do not exist in such rich variety. This book presents not only the achievements of talented jewellers and skilled craftsmen, but also the day-to-day products of ordinary workshops will be introduced.

Grateful thanks are due to all the museums, institutions, companies and collectors who made the writing of this book possible by sup-

8 plying photographs and information and by allowing access to publications. I am also grateful to the following individuals for advice and ideas: Wolfgang Itzigehl, Bantikow, János Kodolányi, Budapest, Erik Liisborg, Roskilde, Jürgen Warmbier, Berlin, Karl-Heinz Syring, Flensburg.

Snuff-boxes

Catherine de Médicis, mother of Francis II, the King of France (1559–1560), persuaded her physicians to give her son tobacco dust to sniff as treatment for the frequent headaches from which he suffered. Apparently the treatment must have been effective, for courtiers also started to take snuff. From the French Court, the source of all new fashions, the new habit spread to the nobility in other areas, and soon also to wealthy burghers and the clergy.

It then became common for priests and congregations to take snuff even during church services, which led to a formal complaint from the cathedral authorities in Seville. Similar complaints flooded in to the Vatican, and Pope Urban VIII (1623–1644) issued a papal bull on 30th January 1644 against the spreading custom: "We hereby use our apostolic authority to forbid, on pain of excommunication, and with the order, where necessary, to invoke the secular arm of the law, all and sundry of both sexes, lay persons and priests, to snuff, smoke or otherwise take tobacco in church."

It was presumably insufficient adherence to this order which prompted Pope Innocent XII (1691–1700) to renew it and indeed to strengthen it. Benedict XIII (1724–1730), himself an inveterate snuff-taker, restricted his predecessors' decrees to the actual duration of liturgical ceremonies and, at the same time, displayed shrewd business sense by imposing a church monopoly on the production and sale of tobacco.

The Republic of Venice also opened up a lucrative source of income by imposing a monopoly on tobacco. Within five years the city state had made a profit of 46,000 gold ducats from tobacco.

Initially, snuff-takers had to use the same type of tobacco as smokers. Tobacco spinners produced a strand of about the thickness of the human thumb from the leaves, and these appeared in the shops rolled together like a rope. The consumer then cut off a suitable length and ground it into a powder. The device used for this was based on the common nutmeg grater. In the 17th century in particular it was very common to grate nutmeg into soups, sweets and drinks. Both forms of grater are very similar, and it is often not possible to separate one from the other; indeed, many were probably used for both purposes.

The powder is collected in the shell-shaped end of the grater and then transferred to the nose with the finger or the hand.

Gradually, ready-to-use tobacco appeared on the market. The Royal Milling and Crushing Works in Lisbon began to produce aromatic snuff, and the name of "Spaniol" soon became synonymous with snuff. Heavy tobaccos from North America, Brazil, Hungary, and Poland were normally used. Each manufacturer had his own method of production, with strictly guarded recipes for the sauces.

Two basic variants can be distinguished: light types and dark mixtures. In the case of the former, hot sauce was added to the ground tobacco; the latter mixtures had various drugs added, for example the flowers of sweet clover (*Melilotus officinalis*), and salt and potash. The mixture was boiled and then matured at medium temperatures before being ground again.

Many terms in the manufacture of snuff are of French origin and were taken over by other countries together with the technology concerned. Typical for French manufacturers was the production of *carottes*, or "carrots", whose name arose because of their carrot-like shape. To produce these, tobacco leaves were dipped in a sauce and, after being hung to drip for a while, were twisted into spiral forms. The next day the carrot was twisted in the opposite direction. It was then hung up to dry on a line for several weeks. When hardened, the tobacco was tightly bound and left to mature for several months. The bundle was then undone, the tobacco ground and stored in barrels. Regular moistening with a mixture of vinegar and alcohol helped it to mature like whisky.

These carrots were sold in France up till 1756, when members of the "Corporation des Râpeurs jurés" took over the grinding process at home.

The carrot shape became the trademark of all tobacco dealers in France. Right until the end of the 19th century shops displayed the carrot sign, made of wood or tin and painted on a red background with tobacco symbols.

Compared with snuff rubbed by the individual himself, pre-rubbed snuff was of a more even, finer consistency. Various different flavours were added to meet all tastes. Strongly perfumed snuff was popular during the Baroque period. Powder, perfume and strongly scented essences were used to hide the unpleasant smells of this period with its rather rudimentary attitude towards hygiene. An idea of how common snuff was is given by the fact that Simon Barber's instruction book on the perfuming of tobacco entitled *Le parfumeur français* was reprinted four times between 1693 and 1698.

"Poggibonci" from Italy was an important example of the snuff of this period. To make the "Grand cardinal" type 100 kg Saint-Omer tobacco were mixed with 15 kg cooking salt and 10 litres of liquid ammonia. In the second half of the 18th century the more refined taste of the Rococo period led to a change in the perfumes added to snuff. For the "Duchesse" type a sauce was made out of cassia (*Cassia fistula*) and sweet almonds.

The Spaniol mixture "Bonbon" was particularly popular among lady snuff-takers. To make it, 100 kg tobacco powder were mixed with 6 kg cream of tartar (*Tartarus depuratus*), 12 kg carbonate of soda, 4 kg red sandalwood, 280 g benzoin, 280 g storax, 70 g tonka beans, 35 g ambergris, 35 g vanilla and 140 g violet roots. For the sauce, 35 g cedar, lavender and bergamotte oil were mixed in alcohol, 1 kg syrup was added, and the whole mixture thinned with 20 litres of warm tobacco wash. The tobacco was kneaded with this mixture and then carefully packed in paper. As soon as the salts, dissolved in the tobacco, began to colour the paper a reddish brown, the snuff was ready to be taken.

Poor quality tobaccos could be improved by adding strong-smelling herbs. In the Thuringian Forest the arnica plant (*Arnica montana*) was called the "snuff flower" on account of the fact that the dried and rubbed flowers were mixed with tobacco. Flowers of the lily of the valley (*Convallaria majalis*) are the most important ingredient in the white, tobacco-free "Schneeberg snuff" which Goethe, no lover of tobacco, was offered by Karl Ludwig von Knebel with the words: "It is refreshing. The effects of the Schneeberg powder are excellent; it

sharpens the wits and improves the memory."
Today the Adler Pharmacy in Schneeberg still
produces the snuff, thus continuing an old tradition. For more than a century all tobacco
sales were a monopoly of pharmacies, and the
privilege was only extended to other shops in
around 1700.

The fact that pharmacies used to sell tobacco
can be seen in the existence of tobacco jars,
which were commonly used for advertising
purposes. These polychrome glazed stoneware
jars were usually produced in Delft or Paris,
and in most cases bear a label identifying the
contents as snuff tobacco. In their form and detail these jars resemble other pharmacy jars.
They were not intended for the personal use of
snuff-takers—they contained several pounds of
snuff. For this purpose a practical container
was developed with a closely fitting lid—the
snuff-box. Early examples, with their similar
decoration, are scarcely distinguishable from
powder-boxes of the time. The only characteristic feature of them was their shortness—
under 6.5 cms. Snuff-boxes did not reach a
length of 8 to 10 cms until some time between
1730 and 1795.

In 1710 the Nuremberg architect Paul Decker
published his notes for goldsmiths, glasscutters
and other artists, which contain the first designs for snuff-boxes. In his drawings Decker
used designs created by the Frenchman Jean
Bérain in the 1680s.

After 1730 the rounded, oval, angular, assymetrical and figural containers appeared.
Snuff-boxes were regarded as fashionable luxury objects and were used to impress others.

Since the Middle Ages, decorative boxes had
been popular gifts for lovers to give each other.
The word *Dose* (box), which had been taken
over from Germanic languages in the 14th century, took on the additional meaning of a "gift".

In the strict hierarchical society of feudal
times, snuff-boxes were much sought-after
gifts used to reward even people low in the social order, who could not have orders bestowed
upon them.

Snuff-taking was part of the etiquette of the
nobility and there was a concomitant ritual of
gestures for the process. The Duke of La Rochefoucauld (1613–1680), whose collection of critical aphorisms *Reflexions ou Sentences et maximes morales* describes the ideas of courtly society, was renowned for the elegance with
which he took snuff.

A French publication of the time identifies
fourteen steps in the correct use of the tobacco
container:

1. The snuff-box is grasped by the left hand
2. The snuff-box is taken in the left hand
3. The snuff-box is tapped
4. The snuff-box is opened
5. The snuff is offered to the group
6. The snuff-box is taken back
7. The snuff-box is left open
8. The tobacco is collected by tapping the
    side of the box
9. The tobacco is deftly gathered together
    with the right hand
10. The tobacco is held for a while between the
    fingers before being advanced to the nose
11. The tobacco is advanced to the nose
12. One inhales the snuff with both nostrils
    without grimacing
13. One sneezes, coughs and spits
14. The snuff-box is closed

Snuff-boxes from Parisian jewellers, who produced individual pieces of great craftsmanship, were much in demand at other courts and
served as models for their craftsmen. Boxes
were produced whose value nowadays is virtually incalculable. In 1764 the Parisian jeweller

Nadet delivered a snuff-box worth 1800 livres; Prince Doria received a box as a present in 1782 which the goldsmith Solle had decorated with 173 diamonds and a picture of Louis XVI and sold for 29,090 livres.

Such extravagance was characteristic of the nobility during the period of absolutist monarchy and had its roots in the political power-shift which was occurring. Luxury was one of the few privileges which marked out the nobility from the rich, but never fully subservient bourgeoisie. At the courts of the absolutist rulers centres of artistic craftsmanship were established which had a clear advantage over the municipal guilds. The craftsmen involved were not subjected to the regulations and restrictions of the guild and had the additional advantage of the possibility of close cooperation with leading architects, sculptors, painters, decorators and technicians.

Snuff-boxes became an integral element in courtly clothing. The flap pockets sewn on to the outside of gentlemen's jackets are supposed to have been introduced so that the dandies could always have their snuff-box at the ready. Often several boxes were carried around. Light boxes for the summer, larger ones for the winter, very large ones which had their place on the mantlepiece, and tiny ones containing just one day's supply for huntsmen to carry with them. One such huntsman's box belonging to Augustus II (the Strong) of Saxony (1670–1733) and decorated with 104 diamonds is now in the art collection of the Grünes Gewölbe in Dresden.

Johann Melchior Dinglinger, court jeweller to the Saxon kings, produced accessories for complete wardrobes that even included buttons which exactly matched the colour and material of the snuff-boxes to be carried. Count Brühl, Augustus II's extravagant Prime Minister, possessed over 800 snuff-boxes, for 300 of which he had clothes to match.

The snuff-boxes produced in the Parisian workshops were copied so faithfully in other places that it is often difficult to identify the provenance of individual items. It is even difficult to date them precisely, as boxes in the Louis Quinze style, for example, were still being produced in perfect quality during the

2 *Packet of Schneeberg snuff. Adler-Apotheke, Schneeberg, Erzgebirge, 1981*

Restoration period or even, over a hundred years later, during the Second Empire. Although these objects attain the same quality as their models, many collectors reject them as being mere reproductions when they come on to the market.

The origin of valuable items made by jewellers can be established not only by examination of their form and the materials used, but also by identification of hallmarks. These include not just the craftsman's mark but also city, customs and tax hallmarks and, since the end of the eighteenth century, information on the degree of purity of the precious metals used. French pieces usually bear four marks which allow the precise year of manufacture to be identified. Up till 1739 a cow as hallmark signified that the object was allowed to be exported out of France. In Russia the double eagle became customary as a state hallmark around 1700. There are a variety of comprehensive works of reference available which enable collectors to identify hallmarks.

Closely related to snuff-boxes made of precious metals are those manufactured by stone-cutters or jewellers in semi-precious stone or amber. These were especially common in German capital cities.

Using Florentine mosaics as a model, the Parisian jeweller Adrien Vachette and the Dresden jeweller Christian Neuber produced boxes with relief mosaics made of cut semi-precious stones. According to the method used to attach the stones the technique involved is called *incrusté* work or *à la mosaïque* work. The decoration of these boxes is the same wherever they were produced: asymmetrical patterns of flowers, fruits, vines.

The work of Berlin craftsmen during the time of Frederick II (1740–1786) displays a particularly high level of creativity. The King, who had a reputation for being very careful with money, had only one luxury—the collecting of snuff-boxes. Boxes from Paris only rarely figure in the estate receipts. In 1740 the King even forbade the importation of luxury goods, including snuff-boxes. This decree lead to a noticeable rise in the fortunes of the Berlin craftsmen.

Among the ranks of these craftsmen were many Huguenots who had had to leave France for religious reasons. In 1700 in the Brandenburg March there were 62 goldsmiths, jewellers and stone-cutters of French origin. In line with their religious beliefs they showed a preference for simple, economical forms in their work.

Many of the boxes produced during this period were designed by Jean Guillaume Krüger, whom Frederick II had brought to Berlin when he was still Crown Prince. The court jeweller, Daniel Baudeson, also a Huguenot, produced many of them. Another craftsman working in Berlin at this time was the versatile Daniel Chodowiecki (1726–1801), who not only designed but also manufactured snuff-boxes.

The talented King himself designed snuff-boxes, which he then had made, using the semi-precious stone Chrysopras which was found in Silesia. The articles produced in Berlin achieved a special brilliance by the skilful use of metal foils with translucent stones and contrasted background and relief work. Another type of box is characterized by delicate hazy colours achieved by the use of mother-of-pearl instead of semi-precious stones.

Frederick II used to present snuff-boxes as gifts. After his death 120 gold boxes set with diamonds worth 1.5 million talers were listed in his possession, of which only a few have survived. A few years ago snuff-boxes from the King's collection were among articles stolen in a robbery at the Hohenzollern castle of Hechingen in

Württemberg. The thieves removed valuable precious stones from their settings and sold them separately from the metal. Six boxes were spared and were presented to the collection in the Charlottenburg Palace in Berlin (West) by Prince Louis Ferdinand of Hohenzollern.

Often the King carried his snuff loose in his pocket. It is perhaps only hearsay that he had his pockets lined with zinc foil so that the snuff remained fresh. Certainly clothes from the King's wardrobe preserved in the Museum für Deutsche Geschichte (Museum of German History) in Berlin do not have any traces of such linings.

It is said that Napoleon Bonaparte also kept his snuff in a similar manner. The French Emperor had valuable snuff-boxes made for his personal use with portraits of his predecessors. One tortoiseshell box bore the medallion portraits of Roman emperors, another pictures of Alexander the Great, Charles XII, Peter I and the Emperor Augustus. A lock of hair from his first wife, Josephine was incorporated into the lid of another box. And Marie Louise, his second wife, was commemorated on the lid of a further one.

As new materials became available to craftsmen and new methods were developed, so these were applied to the manufacture of snuffboxes. In particular, European porcelain now began to be used. Boxes made of porcelain appear after 1730, combined skillfully with gold and miniature paintings. The Meissen factory led in this field. In 1770 boxes decorated with paintings of fruit were sold for 5 talers, and others painted on two surfaces sold for 6 to 11 talers; ones decorated with figures and landscapes sold for 21 to 38 talers, while those with "figures from Ovid and landscapes *en miniature*" cost 34 to 88 talers. In 1777 the Berlin Royal Porcelain Factory made the claim that its products were "2 groschen cheaper" than equivalent products from Meissen.

Frederick II had impressive numbers of boxes made by the Royal Porcelain Factory with which he used to reward deserving officers. After the battle of Rossbach in 1757 all the officers involved were given these as rewards for their victory, or similar boxes in white enamel on tombac. General von Puttkamer possessed an enamel box on whose lid the King and the artillery, which won the battle, are portrayed. On the inside of the lid is a further battle scene and on the base a map of the battlefield. The side bears the following verses:

Storms and lightning may be near
Yet Virtue has no need to fear.
Prudence stands in her defence
And banishes all dangers hence.

Let sun shine down on all of those
Who wish us well, but to our foes,
Whose hearts are false, and wish us ill,
May e'en the moon be covered still.

If you, with toil and sweat and grind,
The way to Honour's temple find,
If some false step is not the cause
Of Fear and Envy, fatal flaws,
Then surely Fame, in future days,
Will give to you the purest praise.

Another porcelain box had in the lid a miniature of Frederick II based on a portrait by the court painter, Antoine Pesne. On the lid an armed warrior is fighting a lion, a leopard, a snake and a griffin. The inscription refers to Prussia's war against several enemies:

Though you attack me where you may,
However many, I shall win the day!

14 Using enamel snuff-boxes from the Berlin workshop of Grimaud Fromery, papier-mâché boxes by Johann Heinrich Stobwasser and tobacco containers from Iserlohn—which are often mistakenly classified as snuff-boxes—it is possible to trace almost the entire course of the Silesian Wars. In his novel *Vor dem Sturm* (Before the Storm), Theodor Fontane describes a collector of these martial snuff-boxes: "Kammerherr von Medewitz auf Alt-Medewitz was a keen collector of boxes. His collection from Frederick's time was almost complete. From the Mollwitz box, which showed the young King being received at the gates of Ohlau with flintlock volleys, to the Hubertusburg box, which showed a courier riding through the world waving a flag with the word 'Peace' on it, he had them all—some of them even twice over."

Another large category of snuff-boxes—which was popular not only during the Rococo period—was decorated with amorous miniatures. Countless second-rate artists earned their living producing such pictures, only a few of which are identifiable by their signatures. The names of others, such as the Viennese artists J. Schreiber, N. Abblati, K. Greineisen, A. Baldorf, appear in decrees as a result of the police authorities imposing a ban on the sale of their snuff-boxes "on moral grounds". One outstanding proponent of these erotic miniatures was Karl Gustav Klingstedt, born in Riga in 1657, who died in Paris in 1734. He was dubbed "the Raphael of the snuff-box" and his many pictures were frequently copied by others. A sliding lid with an innocuous design hid the offending picture. Such harmless sliding lids could also hide politically dangerous miniatures. French Royalists and English Jacobites used these to hide portraits of their idols.

Russian porcelain manufacturers also produced original snuff-boxes. In the 1760s French models were abandoned and craftsmen started to derive inspiration from nearer home. Naturalistic boxes in the form of apples, grapes or shells were produced by the workshops of Veliki Ustyug. The most original type of Russian snuff-boxes were flat "envelope boxes"—also referred to as "packet boxes" in Russian literature—produced in St. Petersburg after 1750. *15* The lids of these flat rectangular boxes carried a dedication or the name of the owner on the outside and the name of the person presenting the gift on the inside. Artists such as Lev Temski perfected the art of reproducing the actual handwriting of the persons concerned. The best engraver was Mikhail Makhayev; the most expensive and valuable ones were decorated by the miniaturist Andrei Chorny, a serf, while Pimen Tupitsyn and Feodor Alekseyev specialized in landscapes and genre paintings respectively.

Compared with snuff-boxes from jewellers' workshops, those made of porcelain were the products of manufacturing processes and were available in—admittedly relatively small—series, which meant that they were within the means of even the bourgeoisie. Enamel boxes are close relatives of porcelain ones. The predominance of white enamel backgrounds suggests that they were supposed to imitate porcelain. In Germany, enamel snuff-boxes were already regarded as old-fashioned by 1770; in England, where porcelain was more rare, they persisted for longer.

Round about 1740 the Martin family of Paris developed boxes made of papier-mâché—fragments of paper soaked in water, mixed with a hardener such as plaster, chalk or rubber and then moulded into the desired form. After it had hardened the box was lacquered or varnished. These popular products were made in virtually identical forms in France, Germany,

England and Belgium. They were cylindrical with low walls and slightly curved lid. As well as the usual clear varnish the interior was sometimes lined with thin slices of dried lemon skin, which enhanced the aroma of the tobacco. These papier-mâché boxes were made acceptable in society by the addition of ivory inlays, miniatures or engraved ornamentation filled with gold dust.

The best-known manufacturer of papier-mâché snuff-boxes was the Brunswick craftsman Georg Siegmund Stobwasser, who received a permit to manufacture lacquered goods in 1763. After initial difficulties the company developed into a flourishing business under his son, Johann Heinrich. Within twenty years, by 1796, the number of employees rose from 29 to 80. At the end of 1772 a branch was opened in Berlin which took over most of the production and even produced pipe-bowls and furniture. Stobwasser's success can be ascribed to the artistic merits of his products. Well-known painters were commissioned and a comprehensive collection of pictures was available for new developments. Talented workers were trained in the firm's own school and received the necessary qualification in lacquering. Stobwasser snuff-boxes are unrivalled for their artistic quality. In 1832 the firm came into the possession of Meyer & Wried, but the name Stobwasser was retained—for obvious reasons—until the firm was disbanded in 1852.

The most important competitors to Stobwasser were the family firms of Ehlers in Wolfenbüttel, Stockmann in Brunswick and Herold in Berlin. Typical Herold boxes had lacquered copper engravings on them.

Another centre for the manufacture of lacquered goods in Europe grew up towards the end of the 18th century in the Belgian watering place of Spa, where they were popular as souvenirs for the visitors. Snuff-boxes with colourful oil-paintings of scenes from the harbour or the surrounding countryside were in particular demand. The realistic detail of these boxes enables them to be clearly identified as originating in Spa.

In 1715 the Frenchman de la Chaumette invented snuff-boxes made of leather, and Thomas Clark of Edinburgh, together with his son, perfected these by adding embossed ornaments and a metal lining. They were popular for hunting expeditions or journeys as they kept the tobacco moist and fresh. Leather snuff-boxes with the inscription "York" came from Stettin; others were produced in Bologna.

The Baroque and Rococo fascination with mechanical devices led to technical refinements in snuff-boxes. One piece of mechanical fun is found in a wooden box decorated with silver which is first mentioned in the inventory of the Prussian Art Collection in 1686. When a spring was released a model of a mouse emerged from the box. Snuff-boxes with two compartments for holding different types of snuff served as models for combinations with clocks or mechanical games. Despite the considerable price of £500 buyers could even be found for the songbird boxes produced in Switzerland, from which a little bird emerged and sang a song when the lid was opened. And further technical developments followed. In 1787 electrophori appeared in England, which stimulated the nose with a weak electrical current instead of with tobacco. These—at first glance rather bizarre—objects bore witness to an increasing interest in technical matters at a time when snuff-boxes were an indispensable element of etiquette.

Even avowed opponents of tobacco carried snuff-boxes appropriate to their status, or received them as presents. An example of this was Johann Wolfgang von Goethe, who was presented with a box by the Tsarina of Russia.

After 1800 snuff also became widespread among the lower classes of society. This spread of the fashion was marked by the development of snuff-boxes made of baser materials and the appearance of snuff in folk-traditions.

Early in the 19th century the Berlin craftsman Daniel Friedrich Loos developed a metal alloy which he called caldarian brass, and he manufactured snuff-boxes which sold for 10 to 16 talers. These boxes can be identified from the hallmark "A.C.L." (aes caldarum Loos) and a head of Hephaistos, the Greek god of fire and patron of all smiths.

Iron foundries in Berlin, Lusatia and Silesia produced cast-iron snuff-boxes with filigree ornamentation which represented an impressive refinement of the art.

Other popular materials for such boxes were organic substances such as wood or horn. In the snuff museum in Grafenau (Federal Republic of Germany) one of the prize exhibits is a sheep's head decorated with silver which once served as a communal snuff-box in an English officer's mess. In Scotland ram's horn was also used for this purpose. In Salzburg, Austria, an industry grew up manufacturing snuff-boxes from goat's horn, usually set in silver. The *Sterzinger Gamserldosen* (Sterzing goat-boxes), called after their place of manufacture in south Tyrol, were engraved with scenes which point to their makers being huntsmen and waggoners. In Sterzing they also made egg-shaped boxes out of horn or bone with engravings or paintings ranging from naive religious, pastoral or erotic scenes to amorous verse.

Small factories in the area around Strasbourg specialized in snuff-boxes made of birch-bark with embossed scenes on the lid. Wilhelm Busch, in his poem, *Die Birke* (The Birch) said:

To make a box
the bark is good enough;
it makes a gift for those
who like to snuff.

In southern Germany and Austria similar boxes were carved out of softwoods. The preponderance of religious scenes as decoration points clearly to such boxes coming from catholic areas. Fine-grained woods such as beech, mango or, in Ireland, marsh oak were also valued materials for this purpose.

One special type of snuff-box was the glass bottle which was manufactured in a glassworks. Similar bottles made of porcelain, glass, ceramic or semi-precious stones in the shape of vases, eggs, spheres or figures originally came from China. It is uncertain to what extent there was any connection between these Chinese objects and their European counterparts. The Asian "snuff-bottles", as they are known in the trade, can be recognized by the spoon attached to the lid, which was used to remove individual portions of snuff. The lid is always made of a different material from the rest of the box—coral, pearls or stone—and is in a contrasting colour. Seamen, traders and Chinese emigrants brought these bottles in large numbers to Europe and America, and they very quickly became collectors' pieces. The captains of trading ships took with them details of the coats of arms of European families, and brought back the finished objects on their return.

Snuff-bottles are still produced as souvenirs nowadays. On the 25th anniversary of the coronation of Queen Elizabeth II in 1977 porcelain bottles with the relief portrait of the Queen were produced, and the state visit of ex-President Richard Nixon in 1972 to the People's Republic of China prompted the production of

SNUFF-BOXES

3 Snuff-box. Papier-mâché with enamel and gold-leaf inlay, in the lid an ivory miniature. The right arm of the figure rotates with the cover and opens the box. France, around 1760, diameter 8.1 cm. Herbig-Haarhaus Lackmuseum, Cologne

4 *Snuff-box with the monogram of the Swedish King Charles XII (1697–1718). Silver, Sweden?, length 8 cm. Kulturhistorisches Museum, Stralsund*

5 *Snuff-box in the form of an abbot. Beechwood, lid with hinge in back, Huguenot work, 18th century, height 11 cm. Stadtmuseum, Schwedt (Oder)*

Following pages:

7 *Snuff-box, enamelled, with playing-card motif and inlaid precious stones, 18th century, length 7 cm, breadth 4.5 cm, height 1.8 cm. Märkisches Museum, Berlin*

8 *Double box with two compartments for different types of tobacco. Copper, 18th century, length 7.5 cm, breadth 5.5 cm, height 3.8 cm. Märkisches Museum, Berlin*

9 *Snuff-box of Frederick II of Prussia. Probably the work of a Berlin jeweller, mid-18th century, length 9 cm, breadth 6.8 cm, height 4.5 cm. Staatliche Schlösser und Gärten, Schloss Charlottenburg, Berlin (West)*

10 *Snuff-box. On the lid the monogram of Frederick II surrounded by trophies. Enamel on copper, Germany, mid-18th century, length 8.5 cm, breadth 6.5 cm, height 3.8 cm. Märkisches Museum, Berlin*

6 *Snuff-grater with sliding lid. Wood with bas-relief carving, Germany or Netherlands, 1734, length 17 cm, breadth 6.6 cm, height 2.2 cm. Altonaer Museum, Hamburg*

11 Black enamel papier-mâché box. On the lid under a clear varnish a coloured oil painting of a monk who is smuggling a girl into the monastery hidden in a sheaf of corn. Probably early 19th century, diameter 10.2 cm, height 1.9 cm. Herbig-Haarhaus Lackmuseum, Cologne

12 Book-shaped snuff-box. Silver, gilded inside, Austria, around 1840, length 7.9 cm, breadth 5.8 cm, height 1.8 cm. Kunstsammlungen des Benediktinerstiftes, Kremsmünster

13 *Snuff-box with blue background decorated with gold
filigree pattern made by the Viennese jeweller Christoph von
Jünger, around 1770. Kunstsammlungen des Benediktinerstiftes, Kremsmünster*

14 Snuff-box from the collection of the opponent of tobacco, Johann Wolfgang von Goethe. 18-carat gold, probably Germany, around 1800, length 6.3 cm, breadth 4.4 cm, height 1.2 cm. Nationale Forschungs- und Gedenkstätten, Goethe-Nationalmuseum, Weimar

15 Envelope box. Enamel on copper, on the lid a handwritten dedication, Russia?, second half of 18th century, length 11.5 cm, breadth 8 cm, height 2 cm. Märkisches Museum, Berlin

16 Two snuff-boxes with built-in clocks. Silver, 1730 and 1710, length 7 cm and 10 cm. Landrock Collection

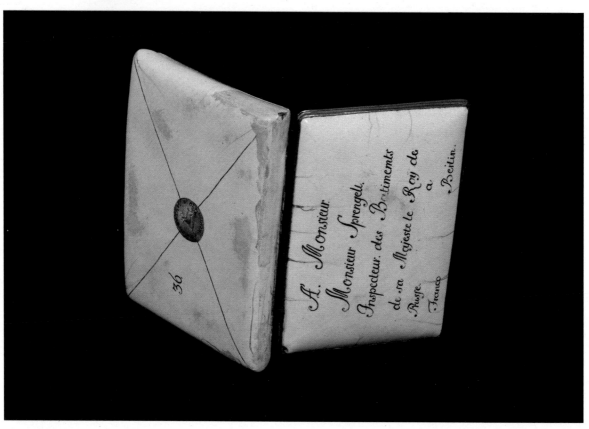

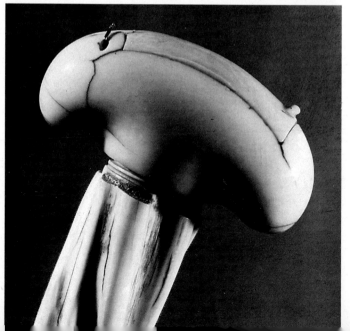

17 *Snuff-box in form of a kneeling Chinese. Enamel with silver fittings, Mennecy, Seine-et-Oise, around 1750, length 6.2 cm, breadth 4 cm, height 4.5 cm. Museum für Kunst und Gewerbe, Hamburg*

18 *Walking-stick with snuff-box in handle from the collection of the Prussian Cavalry General von Ziethen. Narwhale tooth and ivory, mid-18th century, total length 96.5 cm. Nationale Forschungs- und Gedenkstätten, Goethe-Nationalmuseum, Weimar*

19 *Snuff-box in Berlin cast-iron with portrait of the Bavarian King Joseph I (1806–1825), signed F. Detler. Diameter 7.7 cm, height 1.5 cm. Märkisches Museum, Berlin*

20 Sterzinger Gamserldose. *Wood with bone, Sterzing, south Tyrol, dated 1611, length 7.5 cm, breadth 3.2 cm, height 3.2 cm. Schlossmuseum, Linz*

21 *Wooden snuff-container in form of a shoe. Netherlands or northern Germany, early 19th century, length 11 cm. Historisches Museum, Schwerin*

22 *Snuff-container in form of a boot. 19th century, height 6.2 cm. Staatliche Museen, Museum für Volkskunde, Berlin*

23 *Snuff-bottle. Flecked forest glass, southern Germany, 19th century, height 5.7 cm. Staatliche Museen, Museum für Volkskunde, Berlin*

24 *Engraved snuff-container made of sheeps-
horn. Tyrol, 19th century, length 8 cm, breadth
5 cm, height 2.5 cm. Märkisches Museum,
Berlin*

25 *Two snuff-boxes made of birch bark. Southern
Germany and Switzerland, dated 1878, lengths
9 cm and 8.5 cm. Märkisches Museum, Berlin*

snuff-bottles decorated with the crossed flags of the two nations.

European glass bottles do not have an attached spoon and snuff is taken by shaking it out into the palm of the hand. The stopper is also made of a different material, usually juniper wood or metal.

A twist of wire which extends into the bottle from the stopper is used for filling the bottle: a funnel is put over the tiny opening, the snuff is poured in, and the wire moved up and down.

27 Lady taking snuff. Engraving on copper, France, around 1715. Libert Collection

Larger bottles had a twist of coloured wool or calves' hair which was also used to clean the nose with.

Peach-shaped bottles came from Scandinavia, and glassworks in Bavaria produced egg-shaped or spherical *Schmalzglasln* (melting glasses). In the Bohemian Forest glass remains in various colours were melted down and used, the bottles being further decorated with humorous folk-motifs. Sometimes coarse jokes were depicted, like a fat, naked couple standing belly to belly, with the caption: "So near and yet so far".

In Bohemia, snuff-bottles were part of the wedding ritual. The mother of the bride received the best man at the front door with an opened snuff-box or bottle. In Bavarian riding contests the loser received a portion of snuff in a glass container. And in French wedding games snuff was also a common prize.

During the mid-19th century snuff-boxes made from various materials shaped like everyday objects were very popular as gifts. Boxes were made in the form of tools used in the trade of the recipient. The predecessors of such boxes can be found in the *sabots*—shoe- 22 shaped snuff-boxes of the Rococo period —which remained popular for almost a hundred years. In 1800 the two-cornered hat worn by Napoleon, with a pearl instead of the button, became a favoured design for papier-mâché or enamel snuff-boxes.

There were always those who were opposed to snuff. In 1706 the Duchess Elizabeth Charlotte of Orléans wrote to her aunt, Princess Sophie of Hanover: "It annoys me greatly to see women with dirty noses, as though they had—if 27 you will forgive the expression—rubbed filth into their faces, poking their fingers into all the men's snuff-boxes. It makes me feel quite ill to see it." Her fellow-ladies ignored her criticism

34 and competed with the men in the taking of snuff. The wife of the English King, George III (1760–1820), a keen snuff-taker herself, was given the rather disrespectful nickname of "Snuffy Charlotte".

But the opponents of snuff could do nothing to reduce its popularity, which only waned when fashion began to change. In recent years—above all in Europe—there has been a distinct increase in snuff-taking again. Practical disposable containers have replaced costly snuffboxes, which are now more or less a thing of the past.

Tobacco for smoking

In one European country only, snuff-taking was virtually unknown: in the Netherlands. Instead, this republic indulged in tobacco-smoking or "tobacco-tippling", as it was known from the end of the 16th century onwards. Lightly fermented tobacco was swallowed, rather than smoked. Aromatic substances such as tea-leaves, sugar, or vanilla were used to reduce the sharp taste of the tobacco itself. The use of long mouthpieces on pipes also served this purpose—the only restriction on length being the increased fragility and unwieldiness of the pipe.

At first tobacco was only available from pharmacists, but in the latter half of the 17th century specialist tobacco shops developed. Typical figures used as symbols were the tobacco Moor, with a hank of tobacco, the Moorish girl with a loin-cloth made of tobacco leaves, and the pipe-puffing Turk. In seaports these figures, carved in wood, remained as trademarks of tobacconists up to the end of the 19th century.

47, 48

From 17th century Dutch paintings and descriptions of the customs of the 18th and 19th centuries, the clientele of the tobacco shops would appear to have been very similar to that of the cheap public houses. One of the most notorious of these in Berlin was "Der zottige Jude" (The Shaggy Jew) in the Französische Strasse. It was above all during the era of Metternich (1821–1848) that the tobacco shops became more than just places of ill repute and developed into centres for political freethinkers. This was especially true of the Viennese coffee-houses, where one could drink coffee, discuss politics over a selection of newspapers and smoke prefilled pipes, using hygienic removable mouthpieces.

During the mid-19th century anyone going to a tobacco shop had to bring, in addition to his pipe and tobacco pouch, a lighter consisting of a tinder which was made to glow by striking a piece of steel against a stone. In Neustadt, Thuringia, during the 18th century there was a brisk trade in the production of such tinders, using as a raw material the fungus *Fomes fomentarius*. A curved knife was used to cut out the centre from the ragged gills of the fungus. It was then fermented in a cellar, put in damp ashes for two weeks and flattened with a wooden hammer. The pieces were then re-immersed in ashes and water, dried and rubbed by hand until they were soft. This smooth brown "German tinder" was even popular among the British, who bought it direct from Thuringia.

In the tobacco shops glowing wood-shavings were also used or a piece of folded paper known as a "fidibus". The origin of the word may be student slang, or it may come from the French *fil de bois*—wood-shaving. The fidibuses were kept in beaker-shaped containers made of stamped brass or etched, cut or painted glass with motifs related to tobacco. There were also containers made of copper or brass, which held glowing charcoal. Paintings by Adriaen van Ostade (1610–1684) and David Teniers the Younger (1610–1690) show various of these containers with their miniature metal tongs. In a picture entitled *Boy with Pipe*, now to be found in Eger, Hungary, Hendrick Terbrugghen (1588–1629) portrays the lighting of a pipe with a candle. It was not until the introduction of the match, from 1850 onwards, that the lighting of a pipe became a less complicated matter.

Clay pipes

The first clay pipes were manufactured in England at the end of the 16th century using American models. There is disagreement as to whether the first firm was founded in 1573 or 1598. The names of pipe-manufacturers are not known until after 1600. John Stuckney in Wapping marked his pipes with the initials IS from 1603 onwards. In 1635 William Bechalor started stamping his products with the initials WB and a Tudor rose. The number of pipe-makers grew rapidly. Workshops were set up in Taunton, Chester and Salisbury. In London, where the first guild was founded in 1619, there were, by 1650, about 75 producers identifiable by their trademarks, and for the following fifty years 116 different trademarks have come to light. Between 1700 and 1750 an all-time highpoint in the trade was reached with 136 different manufacturers.

Common to all early European clay pipes is the small bowl set at an obtuse angle to the shaft. More decorative pipes were produced after 1625, under the influence of the Baroque period. These had floral decorations in relief or were so-called Raleigh pipes, with the bowl in the form of a human head turned towards the smoker. It is unclear whether these were originally meant as caricatures or a sign of respect. When a flattened base was introduced it became possible to put the pipe down on a flat surface during use.

Large numbers of English clay pipes found their way to the colonies and to the continent of Europe. In 1698 English pipe-manufacturers supplied 2131 gross to Virginia, 100 gross to Spain, 40,970 gross to France and 955 gross to the island of Barbados. Founders of independent clay-pipe workshops came from England to the Netherlands, Denmark and Switzerland. In 1617 William Baenelt settled in the Dutch town of Gouda, became naturalized Dutch and took on the name of Barentz. His short-shafted pipes stamped with a crowned Tudor rose soon made Gouda into the most important centre for the manufacture of European clay pipes. For a while there were 500 workshops here, producing pipes marked with the rose and six-pointed stars. Basic forms with a variety of mouthpieces, 18, 21 and 28 inches long, were developed. Typical Gouda pipes included the so-called *Dorroker*, partly covered with a silicic acid glaze. When the pipe was lit, the resulting heat caused an otherwise invisible picture to emerge.

In Germany, Cologne became a centre for clay-pipe manufacture around 1628. In 1725 the ruler of the principality of Schönburg in Waldenburg founded a guild of pipe-makers. Here apprentices who wished to gain their qualification had to produce, under the guidance of a guild-member, the moulds for a long and a short pipe, and turn out a dozen pipes from each within seven days. The sons of master pipe-makers were given preferential treatment in the regulations: they only had to produce one mould.

In 1753 the sculptor Friedrich Christian Glume founded the first Prussian clay-pipe factory. Further workshops were set up in Salzwedel, Weissenspring near Frankfurt on the Oder and Rostin, Neumark. Around 1800 the 49 workers in the Rostin workshops were producing each year pipes to the value of 19,000 talers, of which pipes worth 9000 talers were exported.

Clay pipes from other sources are so similar to the Dutch models that it is appropriate to make a chronological typology for the whole of Central Europe. Local influences can only be seen in the decoration and in variations in the angle between bowl and shaft. Relief heraldic eagles on the side of the bowl facing the smoker, rows of knobs and a right-angled bowl are typical characteristics of pipes from Brandenburg.

In all workshops the pipes were—with only slight variations—manufactured by the same technique. The basic material used was a soft, white clay with a high chalk-content, which retained its light colour after firing. Large blocks of clay were soaked in barrels, carefully cleaned, and broken up prior to use. The slightest impurity would cause cracking during firing. Brick-sized pieces were cut off by one workman, and another cut these into flat slices which were then kneaded once again. Another specialist took a small lump of clay and formed this into a long thin worm, leaving a lump for the bowl. Often children were used for the rolling process. The next workman took this raw shape, bored out the centre with a piece of wire and gave it its shape in a double brass mould. After the bowl had been bored out, excess clay removed and the seam smoothed, the pipe was allowed to dry before the fine work of finishing was undertaken. The finisher inserted a horn cone into the bowl and smoothed the outer walls with a knife. He then used the saw-like blade of his knife to edge the bowl by cutting a groove around just below the top. With the stamp on his knife he put the trademark or initials of the workshop owner on the plug. Often a second mark indicating the place of manufacture was put on the shaft. About halfway along its length the name, surrounded by several rows of dots, was stamped with a brass die. The glazer then polished the pipe with a glass tube or, better still, a piece of agate.

This process replaced the usual glazing necessary with clay products. Any remaining moisture would cause yellowing during firing, so the pipes had to be carefully dried. They were laid out on a drying board which had a slight hollow to hold them. Firing was carried out using large dishes made of clay. Bits of broken pipe were used as packing. Firing took 12 to 20 hours, and, after cooling, another worker cleaned the individual pipes with wax or soap and polished them with a cloth. Certain pipes were then re-fired in closed containers with the addition of charcoal, which gave them an even black colour.

Individual pipe-makers also existed independently of the pipe-workshops, and these produced short pipes for the local market. In the Slovak town of Banská Štiavnica short pipes called *stiavniki* were produced. Farmers, miners and labourers filled these pipes with tobacco and warmed them in the fire before starting to smoke. In this way less tobacco juice entered the bore—a disadvantage of short pipes, which otherwise did not offer a dry smoke.

The great fragility of clay pipes meant that they became a symbol of transitoriness in art. A still-life by Georg Flegel (1566–1638) in the Historisches Museum in Frankfurt-on-Main shows an intricately decorated clay pipe with a pear-shaped bowl and baroque tendrils intertwined on the shaft. Although even such finely decorated pipes were relatively cheap to produce, hinged cases were developed to protect them. The wide-ranging nature of the trade and uncertainties of supply were probably the cause of such care. Despite being packed in padded wicker-baskets, road conditions were such that large numbers were broken. Prussian customs regulations allowed for one fifth of pipes to be non-declarable because of breakage.

Costly hinged cases with tortoise-shell inlays or carved wooden containers demonstrate that clay pipes were not confined to the lower orders. William III of Orange held smoking parties after the hunt. Modelled on these were the "tobacco assemblies" at the Prussian court. Frederick William I, when he was still Crown Prince, took part in these parties organized by his father.

After his coronation in 1713 he had the splendid chairs in the tobacco room of the castle replaced with simple wooden stools and banned the usual courtly pomp and ceremony. Pewter dishes on the table contained Dutch tobacco, long clay pipes lay at the ready, and in copper pans glowing lumps of peat served to light the pipes. Surrounded by his generals, selected courtiers and famous travellers, the King sat in the uniform of a commander and insisted on being addressed as such. When, in 1736, King Stanislaus of Poland, himself a keen smoker, visited Berlin, both monarchs smoked 30 pipes a night. Only convinced non-smokers were allowed to spend the evening with a cold pipe. A little rhyme circulated among the King's subjects at the time:

When the King's there, true to type,
Everybody must puff a pipe.
Be your title what it may,
That's the order of the day.

28 The Rose is one of the oldest trademarks of pipe-makers from Gouda, Holland. From: Goudsche Pijpen. *Amsterdam 1942*

In addition to the castle in Berlin, the King's castles in Wusterhausen and Potsdam had smoking rooms. P. Christian, L. Leygebe and Adolph von Menzel gave lively accounts of these all-male evenings and the horseplay and coarse humour they entailed. These smoking evenings were used by the King to gain information about historical and political problems, and to discuss religious and educational controversies, and they virtually replaced the meetings of his ministers and advisers, which he seldom attended.

In 1732 the Prussian court provided the model for a tobacco assembly which took place in the

Hermitage palace in the Hesse royal residence of Bayreuth. Tsar Peter III, an admirer of the Prussian monarch, held similar smoking parties. These parties died out with their initiators, but the tradition of smoking long pipes was continued in the annual Bremen *Schaffermahlzeiten*. Since 1545 these fraternal gatherings have been held in the festival hall of the town hall. Bremen merchants, shipowners and captains sit round over simple food and discuss questions relating to sea-trading. It is not known of how long the tradition of pipe-smoking after the meal has been in existence.

In northern Germany and the Low Countries the clay pipe became a traditional gift for lovers. The bridegroom received a long groom's pipe decorated with garlands, or was presented on the day of the wedding with a double-bowled wedding-pipe. In Mecklenburg the mother of the bride puts two crossed clay pipes in a prominent position in the window on the morning of the wedding so that the event can be announced to all and sundry.

The invention of the pipe-rack brought a new piece of furniture into the homes of pipe-smokers. The most beautiful examples of pipe-racks were produced from carved or turned wood in the 18th century in Friesland and Schleswig-Holstein. These took the form of notched racks, decorated with fine flower and bird motifs, into which the pipes were laid horizontally. Monogrammes found on these racks may well represent the names of ladies as well as men, for women smoked pipes too, and sometimes possessed such pipe-racks.

Simple racks in turned wood were made for individual customers by craftsmen on the lower *33* Rhine. Pine boxes with sliding lids, rather like school pencil-boxes, were also used.

In 1803 Johanna Schopenhauer, mother of the philosopher Arthur Schopenhauer, visited England. In her description of the journey she mentions a stay in Holland and describes the smoking customs there: "Tobacco, whether we like it or not, is, for the inhabitants of these marshy areas, a great source of well-being. And there are indeed few Dutch people, from the finest to the humblest, who do not smoke. The women of the lower orders, especially those whose trade makes them spend much time in the open air, the fish-sellers, meat-sellers, vegetable-sellers and bakerwomen almost all smoke. At first it is amusing to see often well-dressed ladies sitting solemnly with long pipes in their mouths. We were told that even elderly ladies and those from the highest classes of society do not deny themselves this pleasure on occasion, but that they treat this self-indulgence as a secret which should not be revealed to strangers."

The traveller expresses her wonderment, too, at the *Quespeldorjes*, delicate spittoons made of porcelain or white glass, which were an integral part of the table-setting in the home and even in the spotless hostelries. No mention is made of another article—a "pipe-sled" made *34* of porcelain—in which the pipe cooled off after smoking. These holders, decorated with pictures of landscapes, fulfilled an additional role as delightful table-decorations.

At the end of the 17th century the production of tin containers for pipe tobacco was started in *35* the Netherlands. The sides of these oval and rectangular tins were made of copper, the base and hinged lid of brass. Their size—12 to 15 cm —differentiates them from the snuff-boxes. A particularly practical variety was an oblong tin with rounded corners which could also accommodate a short clay pipe. Engraved, later embossed, scenes on the base and lid were taken from contemporary graphic art. Biblical, allegorical, mythological and light-hearted motifs

29 *Workshop of a Cologne pipe-firer. Wood-cut, early 19th century. From: Maronde, C.,* Rund um den Tabak. *Frankfurt (Main) 1976*

combined with four-line inscriptions are all ultimately related to folk-art forms. In Germany there was a special tobacco tin industry in Iserlohn. Intricate containers were often produced with a panel on the lid which slid back to reveal a carved picture. Such Iserlohn artefacts would typically carry embossed pictures and inscriptions. The use of die-stamps meant that mass-production was possible. An early Iserlohn tin shows a happy pair of lovers in a pillared hall, the man smoking a long clay pipe. Under the pair there is a banner with the words: *Tabak kann Grillen und Sorgen stillen* (Tobacco calms all worries and qualms). Production expanded during the Seven Years' War (1756–1763), when tins were produced in honour of Frederick II and his military achievements. Craftsmen used copper engravings and pattern books to produce countless tins showing the Prussian King, his generals and their battles. Given the geographical position of Iserlohn, it is understandable that it is mainly events from the Rhine area which are depicted. Probably all the battlefields of the three Silesian Wars are to be found on tobacco tins. Sometimes as many as fourteen are found in a double row on one lid.

The battle of Leuthen is referred to as "Lissa". Almost always one finds a full-length, half-length or head and shoulders portrait of the King, or at least his monogramme. The accompanying verses are propaganda slogans for the King. One tin in a private collection has the following verses on the lid:

FREDERICK WILL ALWAYS BE / FREDERICK, ALTHOUGH WE SEE / MANY WHO MAY TRY THEIR BEST / TO DESTROY HIM. THEY MAY TEST / FREDERICK AS OFT THEY CAN / HE WILL ALWAYS BE OUR MAN / FOES MAY TREMBLE, FRIENDS CAN DRINK / FOR HE LIVES, AND WE DO THINK / HE SHOULD DON HIS CAP AT LAST / AND BE OUR KING AS IN THE PAST

The cheap materials used and the large quantities produced by the die-stamping process meant that Iserlohn tins were relatively cheap and became popular among all social classes. The popularity of these military scenes is demonstrated by the fact that even nearly ten years after the Seven Years' War new stamps with the same themes were being made. Only a few tins carry different decorative themes. Among these are interesting calendar tins marked with important agricultural dates. Inscriptions in faulty Dutch were meant to indicate origins in the Low Countries. Only a few craftsmen revealed their identity through their signatures. One of the most prolific of these was Johann Heinrich Giese, who is also credited with having produced some of the highest quality work. Other names are: Johann Heinrich Becker and Johann Adolph Keppelmann, who rarely gave his full signature and usually confined himself to the abbreviations JAKM, KM or JOHANN A K.

The high quality of Iserlohn tobacco tins is demonstrated by the fact that they were sold in the Low Countries, the country of origin of such tobacco tins. Tins produced for this market carried seafaring or biblical scenes.

The tradition of wrapping tobacco in paper originated in the Low Countries. These wrappers, decorated with woodcuts, had a significance beyond that of the merely commercial. Often miniature works of folk-art were produced, of comparable quality to contemporary prints. As Dutch tobacco had a good reputation in other countries too, this form of wrapping became widespread elsewhere. Even Dutch trademarks were copied. The state only intervened and insisted on proper identification of the country of origin if customs and excise regulations were being infringed.

The larger firms possessed hundreds of copper, lead and brass plates with motifs which were used in their own printing works. The Dutch wrappers tended to stress quality and traditions handed down over the years, and motifs were maintained in order to stress consistency and reliability. Rough woodcut-type depictions of Dutchmen in baroque dress with the obligatory clay pipe are still used on modern wrappings.

After 1800 another sort of tobacco container became popular: round papier-mâché tins with—unlike the snuff-boxes—a separate lid.

From Asia Minor a type of pipe came to southern Europe made of red clay reminiscent of the Roman *terra sigillata*. These pipes started to be produced in Transylvania in Rumania, and in Hungary. By the nature of their construction they can be classified as sectioned pipes with removable mouthpieces. Curved, flowerlike bowls with rich gold ornamentation point to connections with Turkish *çibuks*, but the latter reached lengths of up to 2 m, whereas these were a mere 60-80 cm long. These pipes were popular because they gave a mild, cool smoke. The first line of a song from the folksong collec-

CLAY PIPES

30 David Teniers the Younger (1610–1690), Smokers in an ale-house. *Oil on wood, 33×53 cm. Staatliches Museum, Schwerin*

Following pages:

31 Clay pipe of the Sir Walter Raleigh type. Netherlands, around 1625, excavated in Arnstadt, Thuringia. Height of the bowl 4.5 cm. Museum für Ur- und Frühgeschichte Thüringens, Weimar

32 Two clay pipes. Germany, around 1800. Märkisches Museum, Berlin

33 Wooden box with sliding lid for containing clay pipes. Netherlands or northern Germany, early 19th century?, length 30 cm. Historisches Museum, Schwerin

34 Pipe sleds. Porcelain with polychrome decoration, Netherlands, 1774–1782. Rijksmuseum, Amsterdam

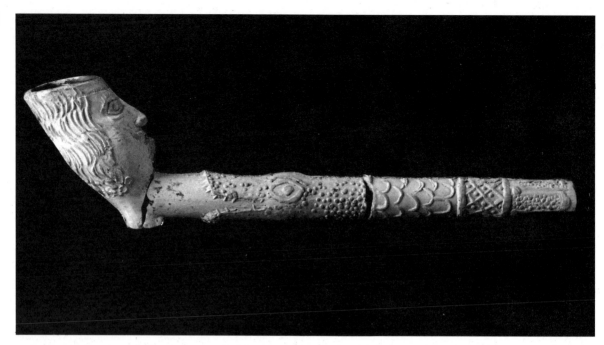

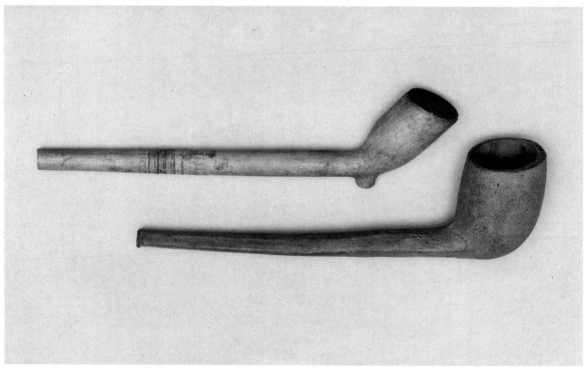

44

46

38 Pipe-tampers. Ivory, Netherlands, 18th century,
heights 6.7 cm, 5.8 cm and 5.1 cm. Focke-Museum,
Bremen

39 Stand for a clay pipe, which is inserted into the head of
the figure. Wood, northern Germany, 19th century, height
17 cm. Historisches Museum, Schwerin

40 *Adriaen van Ostade (1610–1685)*, Smoker in a village pub. *Oil on wood, 45.5×39 cm. Staatliche Kunstsammlungen, Gemäldegalerie Alte Meister, Dresden*

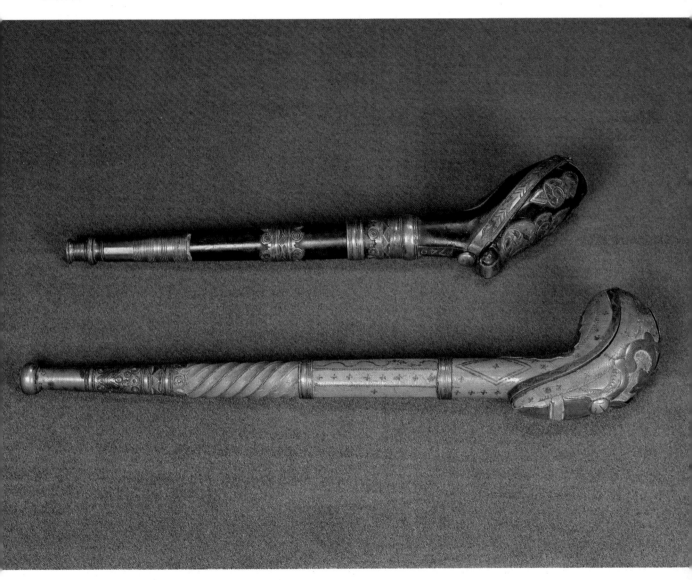

41 *Two cases for clay pipes. Wood on brass, dated 1749, lengths 27 and 24 cm. Märkisches Museum, Berlin*

42 Two pewter tobacco containers by the master
Richard Pitt. The engraving on the left-hand
container depicts a group of smokers. England,
second half of 18th century, heights 14.6 and 14.3 cm.
Victoria and Albert Museum, London

43 *Tobacco assembly of the Prussian King Frederick*
William I in the castle of Königs Wusterhausen. Painting
by an unknown artist, Schlösser Potsdam-Sanssouci

44 *Bowl of a* çibuk *pipe. Red clay with gold decoration. Turkey, 19th century, length 7.4 cm, height 4 cm. Libert Collection*

45 *Napoleon as bowl of a Gambier pipe. Red clay, France, late 19th century, height 6 cm. Märkisches Museum, Berlin*

46 *Viennese coffee-house pipe. Clay with pressed decoration, late 19th century, height 7.7 cm. Libert Collection*

47 *Tobacco negress. Advertisement on a tobacco tin. Wood with polychrome decoration, northern Germany, first half of 19th century, height 60 cm. Stadtmuseum, Schwedt (Oder)*

48 *Tobacco negro. Sign outside a Bremen tobacconist's. Second half of 19th century, height 50 cm. Focke-Museum, Bremen*

49 *Johann Christian Reinhard (1761–1847)*, Friedrich Schiller as a smoker. *Coloured sketch.* *Nationale Forschungs- und Gedenkstätten, Goethe-Nationalmuseum, Weimar*

cop. n. J. Ch. Reinhart.

tion *Des Knaben Wunderhorn* (The Boy's Magic Horn) is well known; the complete first verse runs as follows:

Greetings, old man, how's the pipe?
Show me it—a flower pot
of reddish clay with golden stripe.
Now, for your head?
Just tell me what.

One centre for the production of these pipes was the Birgau valley in Transylvania. Production of pipes, many thousand of which were exported yearly, was an important part of the local pottery industry. Even long after this time, potters were often nicknamed *pipari* (pipe-makers).

Hungarian craftsmen made red and white clay pipes in various forms. In addition to flat *kolmash* pipes, like *çibuks*, there were ones with medium-height and high bowls (more than 10 cm) with moulded ornamentation. These—with usually octagonal bowls—are known as "Debrecen" and "Rákócz" pipes.

Recent excavations in the capital of Bulgaria by the Sofia Museum of History have unearthed over 500 pipes produced in moulds from the 16th to the 18th centuries. Virtually all were decorated with flowers—mainly narcissus or chrysanthemums.

Long-stemmed pipes were kept in wall-racks similar to spoon-racks, which held four to six pipes in a semi-circle with their bowls uppermost.

After 1800, simple clay pipes went out of fashion. In 1832 taxation of pipe-manufacturers was halved in Waldenburg (Germany), but despite concessions such as these the decline of the industry could not be halted, here or elsewhere. The last Waldenburg pipe-maker reported that his wares were sold mainly for annual fairs, where such clay pipes were used as targets in shooting-galleries.

English pipe-makers were inspired by the first World Exhibition in London in 1851. Sales were initially stimulated by putting portraits of people like Admiral Nelson or Queen Victoria on the bowls, or blackamoor heads. Then the latest technological innovations were used, e.g. George Stephenson's famous locomotive *Rocket*; cricketers or jockeys were depicted in relief on the white clay, or figures in black contrasted with the white background of the bowl. The influence of contemporary ivory and meerschaum carving is unmistakable, but the same quality was never achieved.

The situation in France was different. Here clay-pipe production at Saint-Omer was only reaching its peak when other countries had virtually ceased production. In 1765 Charles-Doménique Fiolet founded a pipe-making business in Saint-Omer. When his son took over he employed 700 workers, and by the time the third generation came along the workshops were producing over 10 million pipes per year.

The most superior pipes came from the firm Gambier, founded in 1780 in Givet. Careful workmanship, the use of the purest clay, and tricks such as polishing the pipe with alcohol all combined to result in very high quality pipes. Precise moulds made of metal made production of large quantities possible. Gambier's pipes with their highly decorative bowls in the folk-style became popular beyond the frontiers of France. And they were indeed minor masterpieces of the grotesque and fantastic. All the famous names of the 19th century were caricatured on Gambier pipes—emperors, kings, theatre and opera stars. Napoleon, the Pope, figures from novels, Louis Blériot—the first man to fly across the Channel—all appeared in three-dimensional form.

45

The firm's 1900 catalogue lists 1600 different models. The designers were clever at appealing to a broad spectrum of tastes. Professional people—doctors, lawyers, artists, students—had bowls in the form of skulls and long-stemmed pipes round which a skeleton was twined. In various forms there were depictions of the "true Jacob"—a turbanned, bearded head, the origin of which is explained by a variety of different theories. Some claim it was the Old Testament father of the twelve tribes of Israel, some the Apostle James, others a colonial soldier from the Second Empire called Henri Jacob. A characteristic of all these pipes is a head-band with the words: "I am the true Jacob".

Although the clay pipe was the cheapest type of pipe, it had to give way to other models. Its chief drawbacks, apart from its fragility, were its poor absorption of condensation and the far from pleasant taste of the clay mouthpiece on the lips. In Gouda, Purbeck (England) and the Westerwald (Germany) simple clay pipes are still made to this day as cheap pipes for guests or for testing new blends of tobacco. Often they have an india-rubber mouthpiece.

Sectioned pipes made of wood, meerschaum or porcelain

Although the clay pipe was for a long time the commonest, it was never the only type of pipe made and used. Even Sir Walter Raleigh possessed a pipe made of bits of branches of the cork oak. Bronze pipes were popular among the mercenaries of the Thirty Years' War. Instead of keeping them in cases they poked them down the side of their boots. On long voyages, seamen replaced broken clay pipes by making pipes from the wood of tropical trees or from the hollow foot-bones of seabirds. Even the spurs—necessary for technical reasons in clay pipes—were reproduced, often double, so that the pipe would stand on a flat surface.

Turned wooden pipes appeared towards the end of the 17th century in the French Jura, the area round Ulm and in the hilly areas of central Germany.

In the 1830s and 1840s an industry developed which was to reach its peak in terms of quantity and quality after about 100 years. Pipes made here had a typical three-piece form: a straight stem with a mouthpiece, the pipe-bowl and the curved connecting-piece. Condensation collected in this middle piece, and such a pipe gave a drier smoke and was easier to clean than a clay pipe. In the 19th century the three-sectioned pipe reached the height of popularity. It was confined largely to Germany, Austria and the neighbouring countries, while in the rest of Europe the two-sectioned pipe with the bowl and elbow in one piece was predominant.

The production of wooden pipes in Ulm has been documented since 1733. In Ruhla in the Thuringian Forest it started around 1739 and in Nuremberg at about the same time. In 1747 a hundred knife-makers from Ruhla began to settle in Eberswalde, north of Berlin. With the founding of the knife-making and steel-products industry there, those craftsmen left in Thuringia lost a large amount of their market and were forced to find new products which they could manufacture. Thus it was that a considerable pipe-making industry grew up in this area. Production was carried out largely at home or in small firms with only little specialization, except for the making of the accessories, such as metal lids for pipes or horn mouth-pieces.

The favourite wood for long and medium-length pipe-stems was mahaleb. In addition to the genuine mahaleb (*Prunus mahaleb*), other types of wild prunus were used. When used for pipes, mahaleb wood produces an aromatic taste which comes from the coumarin contained in the bark. For this reason the bark was always left on the mahaleb when it was used. Nurseries in the Burgenland region of Austria cultivated straight wood of the necessary length for the industry.

Another popular type of wood was wild dog-wood (*Cornus sanguinea*). Pipe-makers in the mid-19th century liked to use teak, whose dark colour was excellently suited to inlays of wire and mother-of-pearl. The bowl and heel were also made of the root of mock orange (*Philadelphus coronarius*), which was known as "pipe-shrub", and boxwood (*Buxus sempervirens*), an evergreen shrub from the Mediterranean. Boxwood was very popular because of its fine, decorative grain. For cheaper pipes, field maple (*Acer campestre*) could be used, or cheaper wood was given a varnished finish in the required colour. Often the delicate bowls were lined with tin. A better way of reducing the tendency of the wood to catch light was to treat it with solutions of resin, talc and turpentine. Salt, vinegar and diatomite reinforced the fibres of the wood.

The boring out of the bowl using a two-part adjustable cutter was a process requiring great skill. In various models the heel is not at a right-angle to the head, or both consist of one curved piece. Here it was important to ensure that the bore joined the bowl at the correct point. A special curved drill was necessary for this operation. Around 1850 hard rubber became an ideal replacement for horn for the mouthpiece. The age and origin of wooden pipes are often difficult to establish. Ulm pipes are an exception to this rule, for at the end of the 19th century it was customary to put the words *I bi vo Ulm* (I'm from Ulm) on the piece joining the mouthpiece and the stem. Other hints as to the origins of pipes can be gained from the fact that in particular areas particular models or particular types of wood predominated. Thus in Italy olive-wood (*Olea europaea*) was preferred, and in Finland the root of the dwarf birch (*Betula nana*).

It is said that in Switzerland almost every mountain valley had a different type of pipe. Among the short pipes are the *Schwyzer Älplerpfeife* (Swiss alpine pipe), the *Uechtländer* and the *Maiche*. The *Waadtländer* pipe is characterized by a curved mouthpiece.

It was not until after 1850 that tobacco retailers began to sell pipes. Prior to that time, itinerant salesmen sold pipes which they had themselves bought from wood-turners. Many of these salesmen made pipes themselves and on their travels introduced regional forms into other areas. For example, pipes from Proseč in Bohemia display a close similarity to ones from Thuringia.

Turned pipes are constructed in the same way as carved pipes, except for the products of pure folk-art carving. Turned pipes often had carved decorations added. Animal or heraldic forms were produced using a special cutter. The area round Salzburg produced original wooden pipes whose bowls were carved in the form of various figures—for example a sitting poodle.

Apart from the carved pipes produced by professionals, traditions of amateur pipe-carving grew up, particularly in areas from Franconia to the Alps, where a tradition of folk-carving already existed. Animal and hunting scenes suggest that many such pipes were produced by huntsmen and foresters.

It was probably the skilful hands of a shepherd which produced a wooden pipe which can now be found in Cappenberg Castle in Westphalia. Its stem ends in a carving depicting a man with a lamb between his legs and his arms twined round the barrel-shaped bowl. The clumsy proportions suggest that this was the product of an amateur.

Occasionally, fascinating individual creations can be found, which, in contrast to the normal everyday objects by amateur craftsmen, display the coarse, grotesque form of masks.

In the 19th century an extensive pipe-carving industry grew up in the Rhön area of central Germany. The carving of decorative and day-to-day objects was a traditional source of extra income for the locals in this rural area. A separate pipe-carving profession developed and the finished products were sent to buyers in Ruhla. In addition to using the usual types of wood, the makers selected grotesque-shaped branches and knotty roots for their products, and also the wood of the tea-shrub, which was felt to have particular tactile qualities.

At the end of the last century, bearded heads with the flat cap characteristic of the French army came into fashion. In France at this time, similar anthropomorphic pipes were popular, but in this case depicted a colonial soldier with a neck-cloth to protect him from the sun.

During the German-Danish war of 1864, officers and men regarded the short field pipe as an indispensable part of their equipment. The tobacco pouch which went with these pipes was usually attached to a button of their uniform. In military jargon the short pipe was known as a *Sauzahn* (sow's tooth). A further development of these military pipes was the *Ra-biche*, a pipe with a lid which could be used in the trenches in the First World War because it did not produce any sparks. Victor Rabichon, the inventor of these pipes died in his French home-town of Athis-Mons in 1977. He was one of the few designers of a classical pipe model whose name was known.

A close relative of the carved wooden pipe is the meerschaum pipe, supposedly invented by the Hungarian shoemaker Karl Korvacs. In 1723 Count Andrássy brought back a block of meerschaum from Turkey and gave it to Korvacs with a request for a carving to be produced from it. Inspired by the porosity of the new material, Korvacs made two pipes, one for himself and one for the Count. By chance he hit on the idea of rubbing wax into the pipe. This produced a yellow colour which took on a permanent reddish patina as the pipe was smoked. The original meerschaum pipe is supposed to have passed into the hands of the Budapest Museum, but it is not known what became of it subsequently.

Meerschaum is a magnesium silicate which occurs in white or yellowish lumps in the mineral, serpentine. The scientific name for it is sepiolite. The porous material has good absorbent qualities and can be easily worked. No other type of pipe is so easy to smoke from the first moment—the taste of the tobacco comes out fully from the very start. The word "meerschaum" is a corruption of the Levantine word *mertschcavon*. The Turkish name *lutetaschi* (pipe-stone) suggests that its qualities for pipe-making were known before the Hungarian shoemaker discovered them.

It was not until 1750 that the commercial production of meerschaum pipes began in the traditional pipe-carving areas.

Contemporaries report that Hieronymus Carl Friedrich von Münchhausen (1720–1797), the historical model for the entertaining *Baron von Münchhausen* tall stories, had a meerschaum pipe: "It was virtually only in the company of a small number of friends that he could be persuaded to recount his stories, usually after supper after he had lit up his meerschaum pipe with its enormous bowl and short stem, and a steaming glass of punch had been put before him. The more animated the conversation became, the thicker the clouds of smoke which curled up from his pipe."

Pipe-makers were able to carve this new material with the same instruments they used for wooden pipes. Cutting, turning, boring and filing were the most important processes. Often the pipe-makers produced their own tools. The blade of a saw for cutting the blocks of meerschaum could be made from the spring of a clock or just a tightly stretched brass wire. The main work was carried out with special cutting tools. Eau-de-vie, turpentine and linseed-oil, horsetail (*Equisetum arvense*), chalk and ashes, all mixed together, were used to polish the finely carved bowls. Smooth bowls were merely rubbed with a flannel. The waxy gleam this gave them led to their being called "wax bowls".

There were slight differences in the process according to the manufacturing centre involved. In Lemgo, Westphalia, the craftsmen used dry blocks of meerschaum from which they had merely removed impurities or dirt with a knife. In Vienna and Ruhla the blocks were dampened before cutting. However, these differences in treatment did not result in differences in hardness or smoking qualities.

The roughly prepared bowl was handed on to a specialist who carried out the finer work with a wood-file, rasp, sandpaper and other tools. Then the bowl was immersed in a tallow or wax bath, which brought about a certain hardening of the material. Some producers blew hay-smoke into the bowl in order to bring about the necessary discoloration before they were sold. Sydon Noltze, a well-known maker of meerschaum pipes in Vienna in the mid-19th century, had employees "break in" his pipes before they were sold by smoking them until they turned yellow. His pipes were expensive, costing anything up to 35 guilders.

After 1860, meerschaum bowls blackened either by burning or by colouring were the rage. In the case of the former, the blocks, before they were bored, were first soaked in warm linseed-oil and then held over an open charcoal fire. Soaking and drying were alternated until the material was saturated. The firing of already hollowed-out bowls was more complicated, as these were much less robust. A method of colouring using an alcoholic extract of nuts of the cashew-tree (*Anacardium occidentale*) was borrowed from the button-manufacturing process. A modern method consists of boiling the pipes in purified liquid asphalt. After polishing, these pipes are sold as "goudron pipes" (French, *goudron* = tar).

For their carved decorations—often extremely fine filigree work—the pipe-makers 56 were able to use models and patterns which were often identical for wooden and for meerschaum pipes. However, the actual execution differed according to the grain, coloration, form and flaws of the material.

In 1844 there appeared the *Almanac of etchings*, with four-line verses by Freiherr Ernst von Feuchtersleben and etchings by Moritz von Schwind showing both scenes from the lives of smokers and designs for meerschaum pipe-bowls. Moritz von Schwind's imaginative designs did not just form decorative illustrations for the book; their complex forms were also converted into actual wooden or meerschaum

62 pipes by experienced craftsmen. The motifs represent complete genre pictures. The bowls of the pipes are in the form of stoves, pagodas or even romantic castles. Despite the richness of the detail contained in the romantic illustrations, they do not clash with the actual purpose of the objects they decorate.

The Museum für Deutsche Geschichte in Berlin has in its possession a carved boxwood **59, 60** pipe carrying one of these illustrations—a peasant family grouped round a stove. A woman is playing a zither, next to her an old man with a fur hat is smoking a short pipe. In the centre part the father of the family is leaning against the stove. Next to him there is a small child. A girl is having her hair combed by her mother, and the group is completed by another son or servant.

There are slight variations in detail between the original design and its actual execution. The stove—in other words the bowl itself—is rather more slender than in the illustration, and the icicles on the roof are missing. But the pipe-maker has succeeded in creating his own work of art of equal merit.

Scenes such as this are a rarity on wooden pipes, for meerschaum, as a lighter material, was better suited for this purpose. Sometimes, however, the use of large blocks could lead to over-exaggerations. Surprisingly, it was just such gross carvings which gained much praise for Viennese craftsmen at the London World Exhibition of 1851. Peter Johann Nepomuk Geiger (1805–1880), professor at the Viennese Academy of Creative Arts, who was a self-taught carver, produced an enormous meerschaum pipe on whose bowl 80 figures depicted the fall of Troy. It was bought by an English collector for 2000 guilders.

Towards the end of the 19th century even cyclists were interesting enough to appear as

50 Turned wooden pipe. 19th century, length 120 cm. Heimatmuseum, Brandenburg

motifs on meerschaum pipes. Compared with clay pipes it was much more easy to carve fine filigree details on meerschaum.

Horses, portraits of famous contemporaries and erotic motifs were particularly popular among carvers, collectors and smokers alike. The composer Franz Lehár was presented by admirers with a meerschaum pipe whose bowl was in the shape of a naked girl.

Reeck, a Viennese carver, finished off his meerschaum pipes with a mouthpiece made of amber, thus lending his already valuable pipes an extra aesthetic quality.

In 1890 Kaiser William II had a meerschaum pipe produced by a Berlin craftsman with a rampant capercailzie in silver on the bowl. The head and wings of the bird were made out of stones from the stomach of a capercailzie, as was the beginning of the stem, which bore a carved "W". The bowl was covered with a protecting network of silver wire.

By the end of the last century, there were 150 craftsmen working in 27 different workshops in Ruhla in the Thuringian Forest. A similar number of people were employed in Lemgo and Paris. However, it was Vienna which led the field in production—100,000 meerschaum pipes were produced there each year. In the year 1872, 200 master craftsmen and 1000 workers made use of 360 tons of meerschaum and 30 tons of amber. Within twenty years this had sunk to only 60 master craftsmen with 600 workers. The reason for this slump was not to be found in any change in smoking habits, but rather to be attributed to a deterioration in quality. Often half of the massive meerschaum blocks—which were bought according to weight—ended up being thrown away as debris. In order to combat imports from Turkey, Dreiss developed artificial meerschaum from ground-down debris which was boiled up and

mixed with a binding agent. The addition of lighter kaolin compensated for any increase in weight. It was not until the pipe was smoked that its drawback became evident: it had a much reduced capacity for absorbing condensation. At the same time as this ersatz meerschaum—called "massa"—was introduced, a surrogate for amber mouthpieces was invented in the form of ambroid. Only a few firms survived the loss of credibility among their customers which resulted from the latter often acquiring these inferior products at high prices under the misapprehension that they were made of genuine materials. But a genuine Viennese meerschaum pipe in an appropriate case, like an "Andreas Bauer", is still very much in demand today, and many collectors purchase one of these white "queens among pipes" as a status symbol.

For some years now, meerschaum pipes from Tanzania, identifiable by the small white elephant which is their trademark, have been appearing on the European market. In 1953 meerschaum was discovered near the border with Kenya and a factory was established near

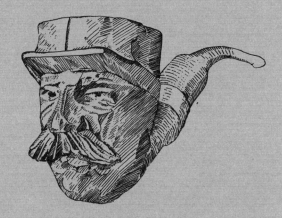

51 Head of a Frenchman. Carved wooden pipe, Germany, late 19th century. Stadtmuseum, Schwedt (Oder)

the town of Arusha which largely uses mass-production techniques, involving 80 different processes, to produce pipe-bowls. Typical for these African products are combinations with bamboo, briar, steel, plastic and leather. By 1967, 200,000 pipes were being exported to 65 different countries of the world. In addition to mass-produced pipes at reasonable prices there are hand-carved bowls with scenes of African animal life. One very popular product was the communal pipe with two long tubes as mouthpieces.

When Johann Friedrich Böttger invented European hard porcelain in Meissen in 1708, this new material quickly gained importance for the manufacture of pipes. The first porcelain pipes were similar to clay pipes. The workshops in Volkstedt, Thuringia, started with the production of sectioned pipe-bowls in 1761. The valuable material was just given a white glaze and very little decoration was added. This tradition was maintained in English porcelain pipes which carried simple, high quality decoration often with chinoiserie.

The porcelain manufacturers produced other objects for pipe-smokers in addition to the actual pipes themselves. In 1765 the Royal Porcelain Manufactory put on offer pipe-tampers in the form of a female leg for a taler each. A Prussian decree of 7th May 1765 forbade the import of "foreign tobacco bowls made of porcelain" and one can only assume that this was an example of protectionist measures by the state; the Royal Manufactory itself produced such bowls.

After 1800 the Thuringian workshops led in the manufacture of cheap decorated pipe bowls. But the best work came from Meissen and Rosenthal. The manufacturers' marks or the names of those responsible for decorating the bowls—who largely worked at home —are only rarely found on the pipes themselves.

Porcelain pipes were at the height of their popularity during the mid-19th century. Tourism began to develop and city dwellers became increasingly interested in the countryside, the lakes and the mountains, and the people who lived in those regions. Just as, at a later date, postcards were bought as souvenirs, so, now, miniature views, porcelain souvenirs and pipe-bowls were purchased and brought home. The porcelain pipe was also used as a present from one friend to another. Pipe-bowls with personalized dedications were used to express particular friendship, devotion or love. Pipe stems decorated with glass beads usually betray the hand of the housewife, but there were also considerable home-industries for this in Schwäbisch-Gmünd and elsewhere.

Almost every craft and trade had its own porcelain pipe with particular decorations. There were simple pastors' pipes with hardly any decoration, which contrasted with long student pipes whose colourful tassles indicated membership of a particular student fraternity. Anyone sitting in a Berlin pub with a long-stemmed pipe carrying a green, yellow and red tassle was undoubtedly a member of the fraternity of *Neuteutonen* (new Teutons). In the university cities of Germany specialist painters took over the task of decorating the porcelain bowls. For many years, students in Jena had their pipes decorated by the painter Eichel with the figure of a poodle in a barrel—a reference to an anecdote about a university beadle called Kahle.

Pictures by Carl Spitzweg, Johann Peter Hasenclever and Johann August Krafft show patriarchal schoolmasters, tradesmen and worthy father-figures smoking long-stemmed pipes,

SECTIONED PIPES MADE OF WOOD, MEERSCHAUM OR PORCELAIN

*52 Two-piece pipe made from root wood.
Probably Silesia, 19th century, length
21 cm. Stadtmuseum, Schwedt (Oder)*

53 Faience pipe-bowl. Ansbach, Franconia, around 1740, length 6 cm, height 5 cm. Germanisches Nationalmuseum, Nuremberg

54, 55 Tobacco pouch made of velvet with embroidery on front and rear. Germany, 1841, breadth 17 cm, height 20 cm. Museum für Geschichte der Stadt, Leipzig

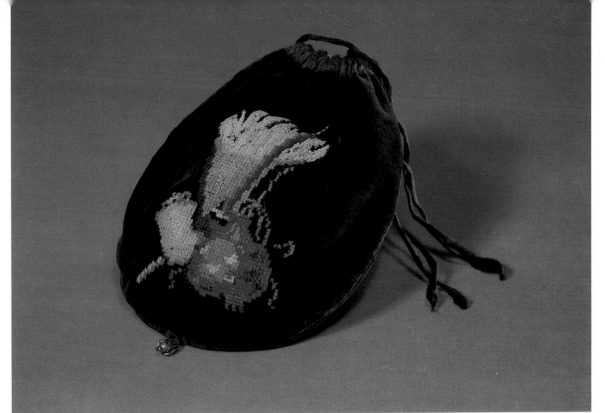

56 *Double page from a pattern book of the firm Ziegler Bros. Ruhla, Thuringia, first half of 19th century, 23.5 × 31.2 cm. Thiel Collection*

57 *Pipe with smooth meerschaum bowl, silver lid and pearl stem, made by Ziegler Bros. Ruhla, Thuringia, around 1830, height 48.5 cm. Thiel Collection*

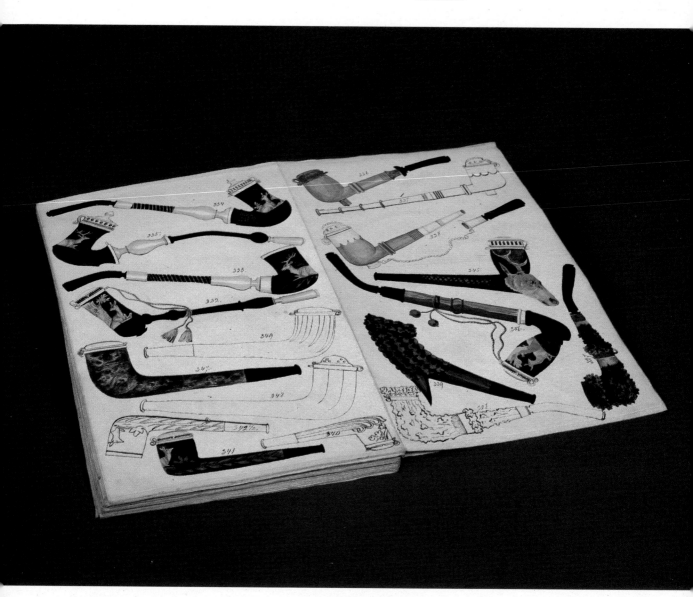

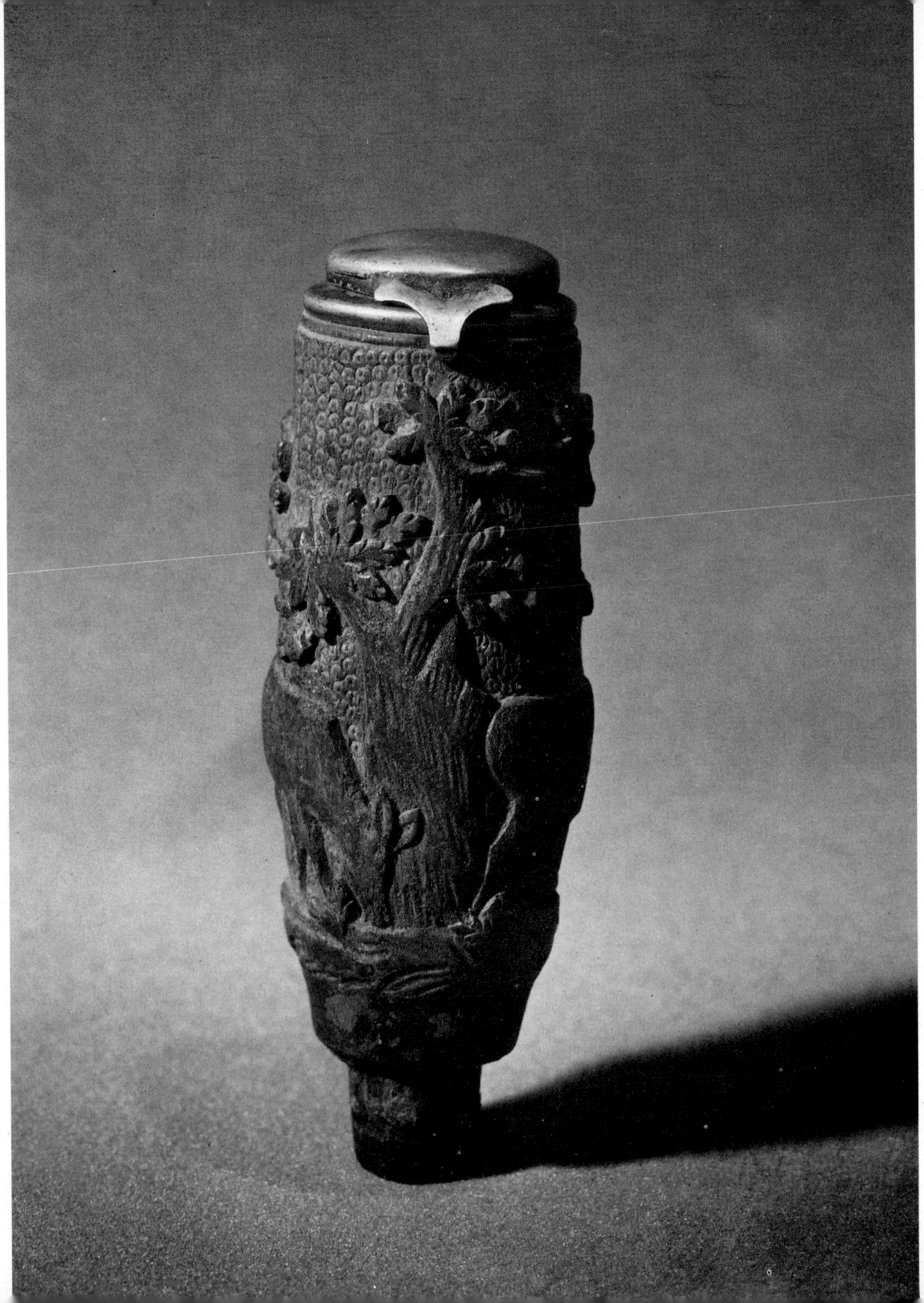

58 Bowl of a three-sectioned pipe. Relief carving with deer in a forest as motif. Northern Germany, probably late 18th century, height 8 cm. Historisches Museum, Schwerin

59 Design for a pipe-bowl by Moritz von Schwind from the Almanach von Radierungen. . ., Zürich 1844.

60 The same motif applied to a carved pipe, beechwood, after 1843, length 37 cm, height of bowl 8.5 cm. Museum für Deutsche Geschichte, Berlin

61 Pipe-bowl made of meerschaum with inlay work. 18th century, height 13 cm. Museum für Deutsche Geschichte, Berlin

62 Meerschaum pipe-bowl with line decoration. Probably mid-19th century, height 8 cm. Historisches Museum, Schwerin

64 Friedrich Moosbruger (1804–1830), The
architect Friedrich Eisenlohr in a circle of friends.
The young men are smoking the çibuk, *the half-
length and the full-length porcelain pipes. Oil
on canvas, 31.3×39.4 cm. Staatliche Kunsthalle,
Karlsruhe*

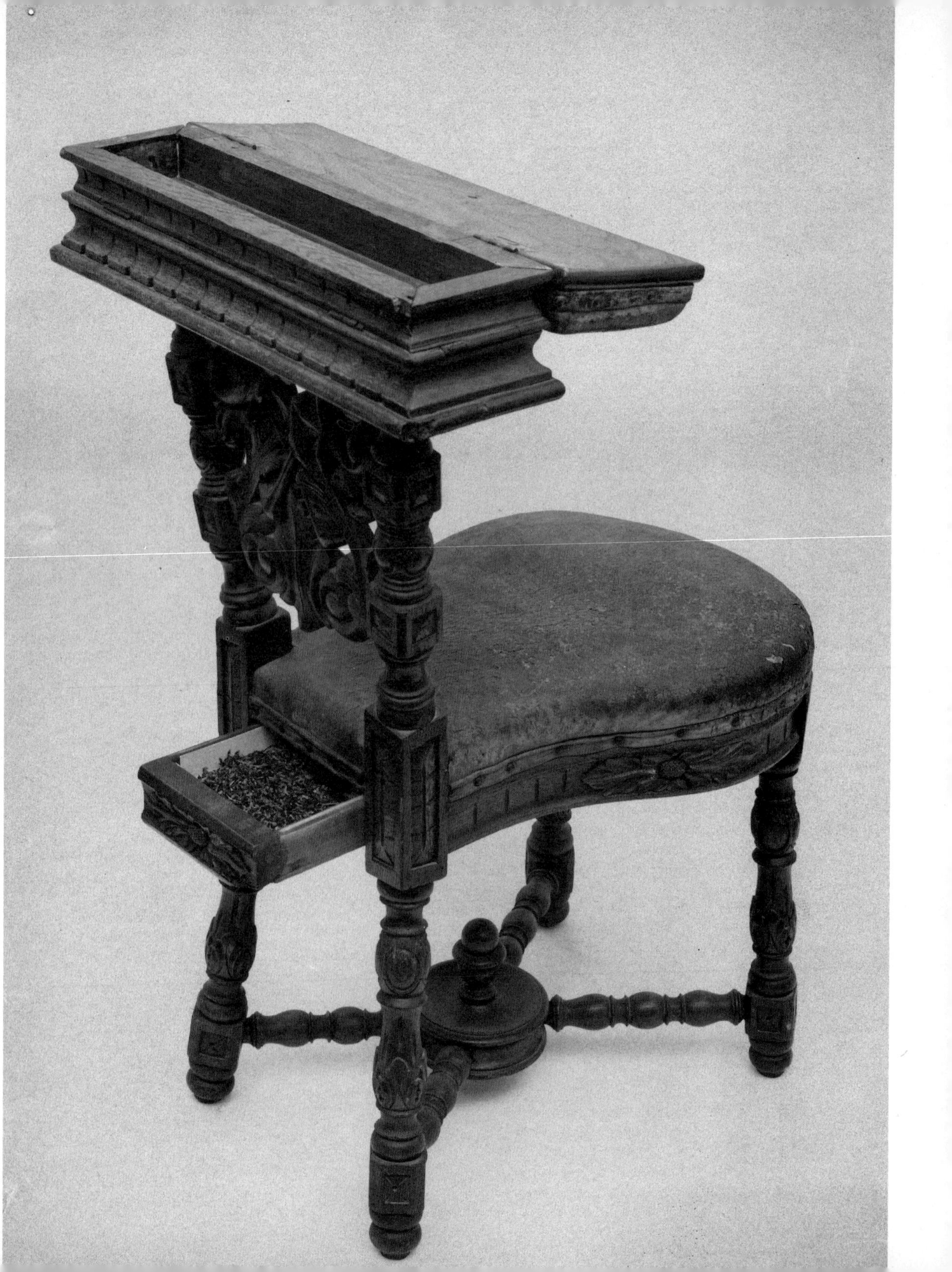

65 Smoker's chair with hinged arm-rest and compartment for smoker's accessories. The smoker sat astride in the chair, which was no doubt used in a tobacco assembly. The carved decoration with crossed pipes indicates the chair's function. Wood with leather, northern Germany, early 19th century, probably based on an earlier model. Focke-Museum, Bremen

66 Dutch pipe-filling machine. When a cent piece was inserted in the slit the lid could be opened and enough tobacco for one pipe was released. Inscription on lid: Voor en Cent stopt u een Pyp Tabak. Wood, around 1820, length 25 cm, breadth 13.5 cm, height 13 cm. Focke-Museum, Bremen

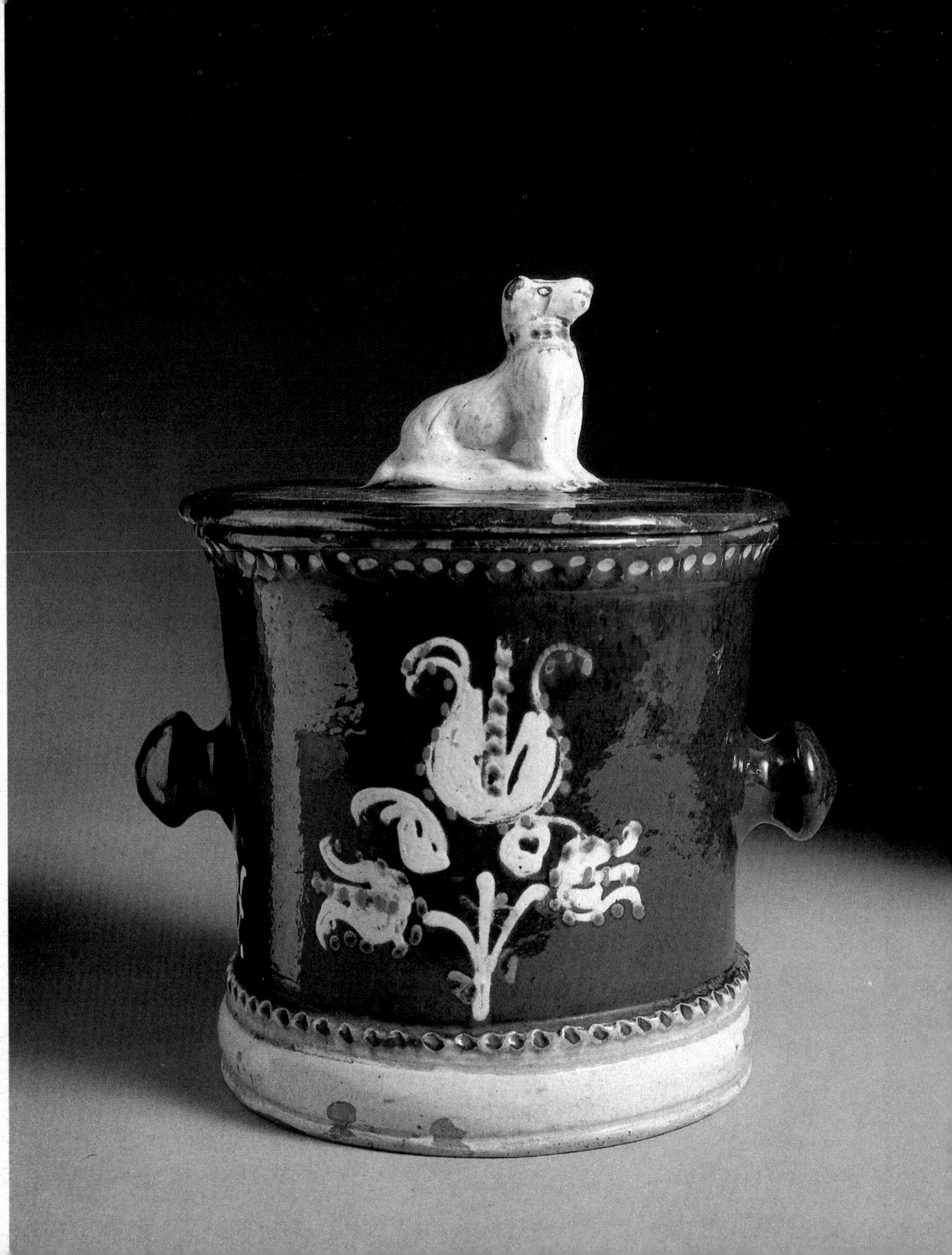

Previous pages:

67 Tobacco jar. Fired *earthenware, probably west-*
ern Saxony, first half of 19th century, height 20.2 cm.
Staatliche Kunstsammlungen, Museum für
Volkskunst, Dresden

68 Porcelain pipe-bowl *with chinoiserie, 18th century,*
height 12 cm. **Museum** *für Deutsche Geschichte, Berlin*

69 Two porcelain pipe-bowls, mid-18th century. Woman's
head with polychrome decoration, signed Meissen, height
6 cm; the other with decoration of roses, Thuringia, length
6.4 cm. Libert Collection

70 Pipe with porcelain bowl, brass lid with sculp-
ture of a smoking Turk, late 18th century, height of
bowl 9.5 cm. Museum für Deutsche Geschichte,
Berlin

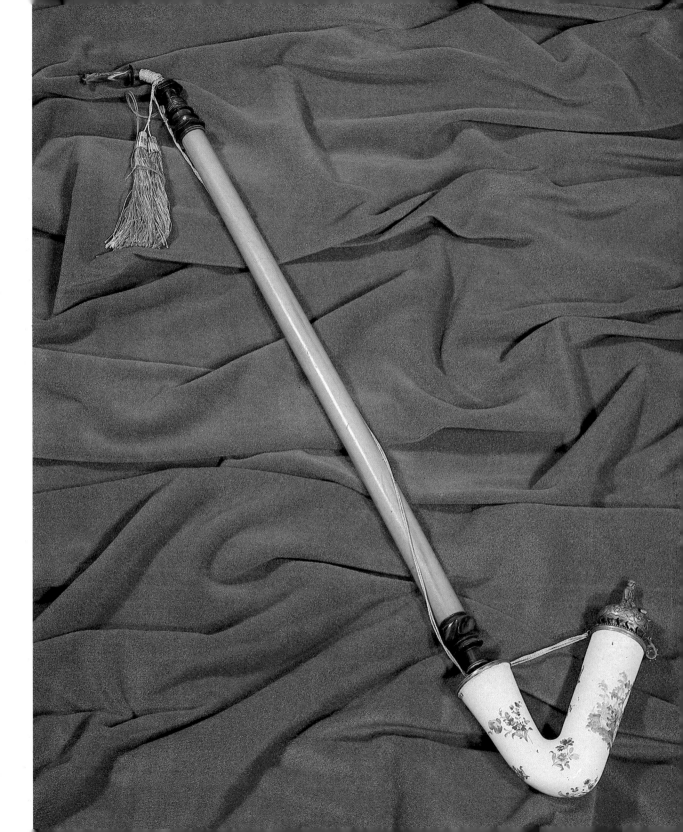

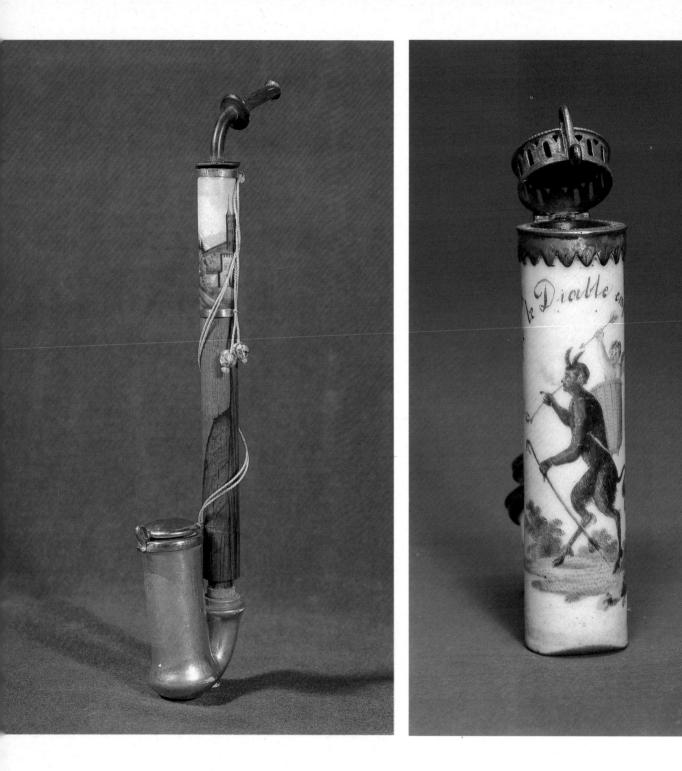

71 Porcelain pipe with gilded bowl. Probably late 18th century, height of bowl 11 cm. Museum für Deutsche Geschichte, Berlin

72 Porcelain bowl of a two-sectioned pipe, silver-plated lid. Above a picture of a smoking devil the inscription: Vive la Pipe le Diable emporte l'amour *(Long live the pipe, the devil take love). France, 19th century, height 10.5 cm. Museum für Deutsche Geschichte, Berlin*

73 Sectioned pipe with porcelain bowl on which is depicted a view of Nuremberg. Mid-19th century, length 46 cm. Museum für Deutsche Geschichte, Berlin

74 Porcelain pipe-bowl with portraits of Francis II of Austria, Alexander I of Russia and Frederick William III of Prussia. Thuringia, early 19th century, height 15 cm. Märkisches Museum, Berlin

75 Porcelain pipe-bowl with coat of arms of the von Osten family. Germany, late 19th century, height 12 cm. Märkisches Museum, Berlin

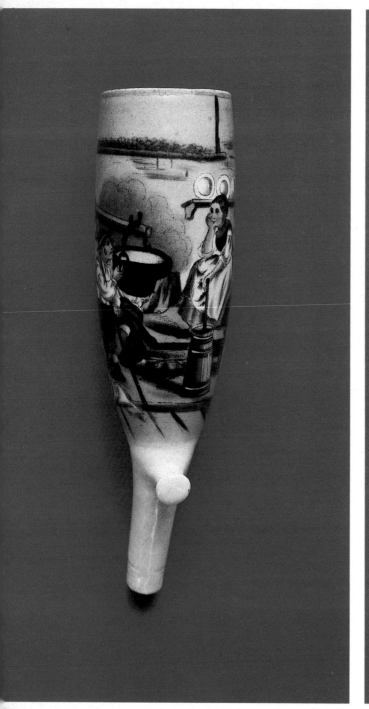 

76 *Porcelain pipe-bowl with depiction of a Tyrolean farmer's family. Second half of 19th century, height 8.6 cm. Historisches Museum, Schwerin*

77 *Porcelain pipe-bowl with inscription:* Wie glücklich lebt ein Oeconom *(What a happy life an economist has). Germany, late 19th century, height 9 cm. Historisches Museum, Schwerin*

78 *Porcelain pipe-bowl. Two hunters looking at two sleeping girls in a woodland clearing. Inscription:* Des Jägers liebstes Wild *(The huntsman's favourite quarry). Germany, late 19th century, height 13.5 cm. Historisches Museum, Schwerin*

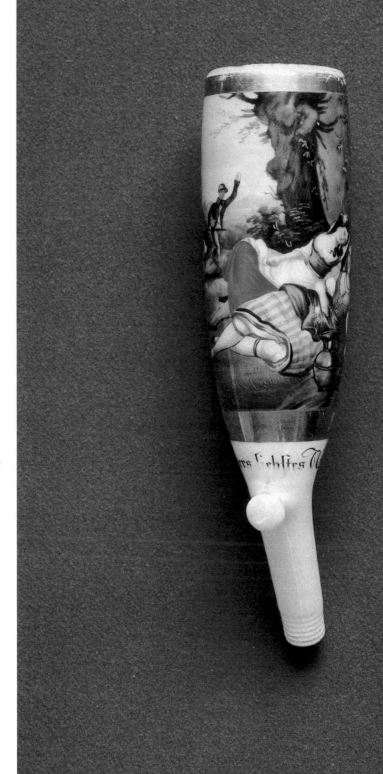

88

79 Porcelain pipe-bowl of a reservist's pipe. On the reverse side are the names of the members of his unit. Tin lid in form of a spiked helmet. Germany, dated 1903, height 14 cm. Stadtmuseum, Schwedt (Oder)

and it was not until the revolution of 1848/9 that such pipes became show associated largely with patriarchal provinciality.

The development of methods of printing and transfer pictures meant that porcelain pipe-bowls could be produced even more cheaply and mass-production techniques used. While the expensive meerschaum pipes could anyway only be afforded by better-off customers, porcelain pipes became popular among all levels of society. During the wars of liberation against Napoleon, porcelain pipes for the first time demonstrated their potential as carriers of propaganda information worthy of comparison with contemporary picture-sheets. Popular heroes like Blücher, Schill, Körner, York or Seume appeared in full colour or in silhouette form on the bowls of pipes and appealed for national unity. One pipe carried an even more explicit message—it shows a newspaper-boy holding the front page of a paper in such a way that the headline about the occupation of Paris by the allies in 1814 can be clearly read.

Later, patriotic "free gymnasts" with black, red and gold flags, and the fighters of the barricades were painted onto the white porcelain. During the Prussian-German wars of unification between 1864 and 1871, the decoration of pipes reached a lowpoint in trivialization and distortion. Between 1864 and 1866 pipe-bowls with a picture of the supreme commander Count von Wrangel sold well. Later, when General von Prittwitz took over command, sales fell. The producers then simply changed the name under the picture of "von Wrangel" into "von Prittwitz". In 1870 soldiers fighting in France received Christmas parcels which contained, among other gifts, pipes with the following inscription: "Christmas/Berlin/relief organization of the German armies in the field/ 1870". During the First World War, porcelain pipes from the Royal Porcelain Manufactory in Berlin bore the motif of the Iron Cross and the soldiers of the alliance. A small black cross on the glaze—the so-called war-mark—identifies these pipes which were produced between 1914 and 1918.

In addition to these short marching pipes, a typical German military pipe was the reservist's pipe, which could reach lengths of up to 1.5 metres. These colourful, heavily ornate pipes displayed the characteristics of the particular weapon borne by the owner. Thus the bowl was shaped like a spiked helmet or a cannon. On the back of the bowl the name of the member of the unit concerned was written.

The German writer, Ehm Welk, in his semi-autobiographical novel *Die Lebensuhr des Gottlieb Grambauer* (Gottlieb Grambauer's life-

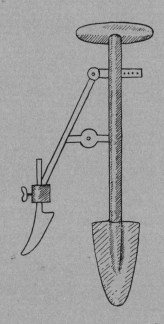

80 Special boring instrument for meerschaum pipe-bowls. Thuringia, second half of 19th century. From: Tomasek, J.M., Die Pfeifen-Industrie. Weimar 1878

clock) writes about the political significance of the pipe-bowls. He is referring to the time after the fall of the Chancellor Otto von Bismarck in March 1890: "My pipe-bowl bore a portrait of the new Kaiser—it had been produced when he first acceded to the throne, and almost everyone who smoked in Kummerow had bought one. I immediately put this pipe aside and bought one with Bismarck on it in Randemünde. Later I had to order two dozen more such pipes. Everyone wanted to keep the memory of Bismarck alive and show the Kaiser that they were not to be trifled with. Yes—that's what Pomeranian peasants did when they wanted to rebel."

In Germany porcelain pipes took on a special significance as denoters of social rank and group loyalty which went beyond their significance as mere smoking artefacts. Gymnastic enthusiasts had pipes with the letter "F" on them repeated four times, denoting their motto: *Frisch, fromm, fröhlich, frei* (fresh, pious, happy and free). Tradesmen had pipes bearing the tools of their trade. The newly organized working-class followed the example of the middle-class associations and displayed their leaders on the bowls of their pipes. By today's standards, the vast majority of such paintings can be classified as kitsch. But for a large number of smokers this was the only form of art which they could afford. Besides there were also genuine works of miniature art, such as representations of huntsmen, poachers and Tirolean mountain farmers, which are rich in naturalistic detail. The dividing line between real art and kitsch is a fine one, for the artists involved were creating, each according to his skill and the wishes of his customer, objects for practical use and not for collectors. When a pipe bears a picture of two huntsmen looking at a woman in a woodland glade and the inscription is, "The huntsman's favourite quarry", then this must

81 *Design for a meerschaum pipe-bowl by Moritz von Schwind from the* Almanach von Radierungen. . ., *Zürich 1844*

be seen as an example of the considerable number of pipes which can be classified as porcelain frivolities.

Only very few of the excellent craftsmen who produced these pipes are known by name. Examples of these are Lorensz Riemek of Ilmenau or Otto Spliedt of Burg.

After the campaigns of 1813–1815, Marshall Blücher received from friends an original porcelain pipe which was probably produced in Paris. On the bowl was an equestrian portrait of Frederick II. The inside of the double lid hid a small gilded figure of Napoleon which stood up when the lid was opened. Parisian craftsmen were also responsible for producing figured bowls in the shape of Napoleon seated on a tree stump. The hinged head of the Emperor serves as the lid.

Dutch wine-pipes are an interesting curiosity. Here the smoke was sucked through a container which was filled with wine. These decorative porcelain pipes were difficult to operate and did not give a very enjoyable smoke. The development of such pipes led nowhere, but was an attempt to find a type of pipe which would give a refined, mild smoke. Porcelain does not absorb condensation, and continued smoking of such pipes, which became hotter and hotter as one went on, was more of an ordeal than a pleasure. Only the large-bowled, long, sectioned pipes gave a cool smoke. The long stem cooled the smoke and lessened the bitterness of the only lightly fermented tobacco. The smoker had to be careful to draw shallowly only four or five times a minute while keeping the ash down with his stopper so that it absorbed some of the condensation.

Porcelain pipes are still produced in considerable numbers to this day. The biggest exporter is the Czech firm Koh-i-noor. Like long wooden pipes, they are largely meant as collectors' pieces or for decoration of rustic holiday homes.

In Germany, domestic tobacco production expanded during the blockade by Napoleon. Bremen developed into a centre for the tobacco industry. In Cologne, the firm Neuerburg was founded.

In Berlin, popular makes were produced by Ermeler, Praetorius and Brantzlow, or dealers imported products by barge from the Hamburg firm of Justus Friedrich. Smokers had a choice of various types—Cubacanaster, Dutch Canaster, Louisiana Rothsiegel or Muffcanaster—ranging in price from 12 groschen to $2^1/_2$ talers per pound. At 2 groschen per pound, Kraus tobacco was the cheapest and lowest quality. The advertising slogan for Huntsman's Canaster was: "Gives a good smoke in the open air and on the mountain tops. This tobacco burns well, tastes good and is not bitter".

Decorative pipes were carefully displayed on stands. In the north of Germany, the pipe-rack was a typical piece of domestic furniture. It consisted of a corner board with a curved base and a drawer for keeping accessories in. Similar objects were built by craftsmen in Denmark and Sweden. Another method of storing pipes was on a table whose top had holes for the insertion of long-stemmed pipes. Special smokers' chairs provided room for all the accessories required for the smoker's various rituals. The pipe-cabinet, designed as it was to contain a large number of pipes, marked the transition to the collecting of pipes as a hobby in itself. One 19th-century nobleman from Saxony had a large collection which is now to be found in the museum in Waldenburg. An attempt has been made to preserve the way in which it has been collected and the pipes are displayed in their original condition.

Pipes with cooling systems

Many materials were tried out in the search for pipes which offered a light, dry and cool smoke. Some experiments were in vain, others merely produced new problems but were important stages in the development of modern pipes.

The Persians solved the problem of how to achieve a cool smoke by inventing the water-pipe, in which the smoke is drawn through a cooling water bath. To the European smoker these pipes, which require an even drawing of smoke through the long, flexible mouthpiece, seem rather complicated, but they are still popular in eastern countries. In his humorous

65

117

travelogue *The Innocents Abroad*, Mark Twain comes out strongly against such pipes:

"I took one blast at it, and it was sufficient; the smoke went in great volume down into my stomach, my lungs, even into the uttermost parts of my frame. I exploded one mighty cough, and it was as if Vesuvius had let go. For the next five minutes I smoked at every pore, like a frame house that is on fire on the inside. Not any more narghili for me."

Care has to be taken when drawing on a water-pipe. If one draws in the smoke too strongly one ends up swallowing water; if one does not draw strongly enough, one only breathes in air.

In Europe, the water-pipe only spread into the Balkan states which had once been under Turkish occupation. In other countries water-pipes were acquired largely only by collectors. Their attraction lay in their decorative nature, which made them the centrepiece of a person's home. The curved water-containers made of burnished brass, ostrich eggs, coconuts or enamelled glass and faience, often with filigree work round the mouthpiece, are superb works of oriental art.

For those who like this method of smoking, the Milan firm of Savinelli offers for sale small table water-pipes with a simple body made of briar.

86 Round about 1750 in Staffordshire, snake pipes were developed, whose long stem (up to 4 metres) served to cool the smoke. The coiled pipes were made of earthenware. They are remarkable if for no other reason that it was possible to retain the exact bore despite their being tightly coiled. The simpler examples had the stem coiled up like a garden hose. Others had more animal-like twists and coils and, with the appropriate colouring, proved worthy of the name snake pipe.

Even glass was used for pipes. Victorian glassblowers in Bristol and Nailsea (England) 91 produced simple glass pipes with clear, uncomplicated lines. Rings of bosses formed decorations and also served as reinforcements. The pipes were either left in the natural colour of the glass or they were coloured a pastel lilac colour. Venice produced glass pipes with sophisticated blown decorations. Although it was perfectly possible to smoke these pipes, they were usually meant as an original form of joke. Schnapps glasses in the form of pipes were also produced.

Glassworks in Austria-Hungary experimented at the start of the 19th century with coloured glasses. In 1803 a type of sealing-wax like glass was developed and marketed under the name of "Hyalith". In 1817, copying the fashion for black Wedgwood porcelain, black Hyalith appeared. Friedrich Egermann (1777–1866) succeeded, in 1828, in discovering a type of glass which had a marbled effect and looked remarkably like stone. This "stone-glass" was 87 also used to make pipe-bowls, but these had all the disadvantages of porcelain pipes and were even heavier.

At the other end of the scale were corn-cob 100 pipes, which were extremely light indeed. These were first developed by American farmers for their own use. The nickname "Missouri meerschaum" soon became a trade name for such pipes, and they became popular in Europe too. A type of maize called "Collier seed" with a solid stalk was used, and the resulting pipes gave a pleasantly cool smoke. These "10-cent pipes" became popular on account of their low weight and price. But corn-cob pipes only have a short life. When the inner wall of the bowl, with its thin protective layer of plaster, will not absorb any more condensation, the pipe has served its day and can be discarded.

82 Varieties of pipes and pipe-smokers. Lithograph
by J. Grandville. France, around 1830, 25×36 cm.
Märkisches Museum, Berlin

Friedrich Gerstäcker worked for several years with a manufacturer cutting reeds for the mouthpieces of these pipes. Nowadays there is a sizeable industry in Washington, Missouri, producing annually several million corn-cob pipes for domestic and export markets. After harvesting, the large, woody cobs are stored for several years, then sawn, bored and polished. The heel and mouthpiece are today made of plastic, bamboo or wood which is stained to the correct colour.

At the end of the last century, another natural product became important for the pipe industry: the African calabash (*Lagenaria siceraria*). The first trumpet-shaped, large-bowled calabash pipes probably reached Europe during the Boer War. These light pipes were then completed by the addition of a meerschaum lining and an amber mouthpiece. As these pipes have a space between the inside and outside walls of the bowl, they offer a very mild smoke. In the USA the calabash pipe was adapted as a

"General Daves Pipe", which had a stem attached near the top of the double-walled bowl.

Certain regional pipe forms whose wooden parts are decorated with metal are of interest. The Slavs in particular produced superb creations of this kind. Decorative punched intertwinings, circles or zig-zag lines are typical decorations to be found on U-shaped wooden pipes from the White Sea region. Polish "Goral" pipes from the High Tatra have little chains attached to the curved pine mouthpiece. Each of these pipes was produced—and usually also used—by one individual and so no one is similar to another—apart, that is, from ones which were mass-produced for the souvenir trade.

Modern Soviet pipes are made in a long tradition of folk-art. The state ivory-carving centre in Arkhangelsk produces various models, mainly for export, whose form is reminiscent of folk-art from the northern peoples of the Soviet Union. The jeweler D. Sanzhiyev derived inspiration from Buryat folk-art for his pipe creations which have inset decoration of silver, coral and amber.

Briar pipes

Round about the middle of the last century a French pipe-maker travelled to Corsica to visit the birthplace of Napoleon, of whom he was an admirer. While on the island he lost his meerschaum pipe and requested a local farmer to make him a new pipe out of any suitable type of wood. The next day he was presented with a carved pipe bowl made of the root of a type of heath. The Frenchman tried this new pipe out, was impressed by its qualities and founded a briar-pipe making industry in the little town of Saint-Claude. So the story goes. It seems likely that Corsican shepherds had already at an earlier date started using the hard roots of the plant for making pipes, and French traders took over the material from them. The heath (*Erica arborea*) which is suitable for making pipes is only to be found in the Mediterranean region, where it grows to heights of up to several metres. The plant grows wild in Tunisia, Morocco, southern France, Greece, Albania and on the islands of Corsica and Sardinia. All attempts to cultivate the plant have hitherto failed. Even in Florida, under optimum conditions, the Americans failed to domesticate the plant. Types of heath native to that part of the world do provide roots, but the wood of these is inferior, and pipes made of this "breezewood", as it was called, did not sell in Europe.

By comparison with other types of wood, briar root, as it is called in English, is particularly robust. It also has a pleasant taste and excellent aesthetic qualities. Modern high-quality pipes are almost exclusively made of briar. The wood is still collected in the traditional manner. The shrubs grow up to heights of 5 metres, but all that is used is the burr between the trunk and the root. These lumps only reach a weight of 10 kilogrammes or more when the plant reaches the age of 30 to 60 years. At the onset of winter the burrs are dug up, cleaned and stored for ten months in ditches, protected from the sun by a layer of twigs or cloths. In order to prevent the wood splitting, the hard burrs are regularly sprayed with water. They gradually dry out from the centre outwards, and can then be sawn up into the usual blocks. Years of experience and a natural feel for the material enable the cutters to produce as large blocks as possible of consistent quality. By this stage the quality of the finished product is largely determined. The size and grain dictate the price of the blocks, which are boiled for several hours in copper vessels so that any remaining resin is removed. It is during this process that the blocks take on the reddish colour which is typical for briar pipes. There are also pinkish or yellow variants, and the blocks therefore have to be sorted according to colour, size and quality before they are passed on to actual pipe-makers. Experts differentiate between over 30 varieties and the packages are marked accordingly. Groups of letters denote the place of origin and quality, Roman numerals the colouring, Arabic numerals the size. The highest prices are paid for blocks with a consistent, even grain.

In the workshop the blocks are subjected to as many as 80 separate processes before the finished product emerges. The block is cut, the bowl bored and milled, and the heel turned. A large proportion of all these processes has to be carried out by hand. Machines are used for boring, cutting, milling and polishing, but always under the watchful eye of specialists. The greater the amount of hand work carried out, the more individual the pipe becomes—and the higher the price.

The highest quality pipes with the best grain are left in their natural colouring. Otherwise it is customary for the wood to be stained so that the natural colouring is intensified. In addition to reddish-brown stains, black is also common. The latter are used as highly polished pipes for social occasions such as theatre visits or suchlike, where a degree of formality in dress is required. The black staining makes it possible for tiny flaws to be concealed.

Another finish can be given to the pipe by sand-blasting. At first the raw bowls are put in a hot sandbath. Here the denser parts of the grain harden, while the softer parts of the wood contract and are removed by the sand-blasting. The resulting relief effect produces pipes which are of the same quality as the solid ones but which are lighter, easier to hold and give a mild smoke, thanks to their greater surface area. The Italian firm of Savinelli produces one type of relief pipe from a rare variety of light-coloured briar root, which it calls *corallo di mare* (sea coral). These pipes come very close to having the smoking qualities of meerschaum pipes. They don't need to be "broken in", and

99

83 *In front of tobacconists' shops the shopkeepers displayed their various wares in such a way as to attract customers. From:* Feinhals, J., Der Tabak in Kunst und Kultur. *Cologne, 1926*

gradually change their colour similar to meerschaum pipes.

Blocks which contain flaws are given a relief effect with the milling machine. These second-class relief pipes, unlike the sand-blasted models, are given the classification "rustica" in the shops.

Of course it is clear that the grain of the briar pipe does not affect its smoking qualities, but this type of pipe is anyway a practical smoking-instrument. The warm, polished wood gives the smoking ritual an almost sensual pleasure. *84* The Soviet writer Ilya Ehrenburg, with satirical exaggeration, praised the pipe as being a "strongly spiritual object". In 1922 his collection of short stories, *13 pipes*, appeared, in the foreword to which he wrote: "Scarred and burnt out, it represents, as it were, human existence, a chronicle of man's passions, for in the wood, the clay or the stone are the traces of the human breath."

In the last 30 years of the 19th century—under the influence of English customers—new, simple forms developed for pipes, and have remained dominant for over a hundred years. The designers of models which have now become classics are seldom known by name. One exception is Jean Baptiste Choquin, who, in 1900, incorporated a hollowed-out bone of an albatross in the stem of a briar pipe. The Choquin pipe—originally produced in commercial quantities in Metz—is a standard model produced in Saint-Claude, although the middle piece is now made of plastic, rather than bone.

Of the 14,000 inhabitants of the small town, over 5000 were, at the turn of the century, employed in about one hundred workshops in the pipe-industry. The introduction of mechanization and the transfer of some firms to other areas reduced these figures to 1500 in 40 enterprises. In the years of prosperity 30 million briar pipes were produced annually, the majority of which went to England for finishing.

The words "London style" on pipes produced on the continent still bears witness to the prestige associated with British briar pipes for almost a hundred years now. From England there came the trend in handicrafts—including pipe-making—towards simple, practical forms appropriate to the materials used. The compact cube-shaped pipes resulted from efforts to produce industrialized shapes and these, in turn, had an effect on art. Painters were inspired by the simple pipes; Vincent van Gogh, Juan Gris and Pablo Picasso produced still-lifes in which tobacco pipes have a symbolic significance. Ehrenburg wrote from Paris that he had acquired such a pipe. The concentration on practical forms led to a tendency in art for individual objects to gain almost fetish-like symbolic qualities, and the pipe was typical of this tendency. Poets mentioned them, and for feminists an elegant briar pipe was almost as important as a boyish haircut. The painting, *The Extreme*, by Sacha Zaliuk illustrates this: a woman in a man's suit, with a tie and smoothed-down hair parted in the centre, is lifting a pipe to her lips with long, elegant fingers.

One of the founders of the British pipe empire was Alfred Dunhill, who opened a small pipe-shop in the fashionable London quarter of St James's in 1907. He offered to the public carefully selected quality pipes of simple—now classic—lines. His trademark—a small white dot—soon became known to connoisseurs as a guarantee of quality. Dunhill only used briar blocks of the best quality. He proved his skill as a businessman and psychologist by developing special tobacco blends to suit his excellent pipes, blends for particular times of day, and even smoker's toothpaste. Dunhill pipes still retain their pre-eminent position—which is reflected in their price. More or less all pipes carrying the guarantee "London made" are profiting from the image built up by Dunhill.

"London" is the name given on the continent to a type of pipe which was originally called "Billiard" and must be one of the most conservative briar pipes. The type called "Pot" is flatter and broader. "Dublin", with its angled bowl, and "Liverpool", with its narrowing bore, are variants. "Apple" and "Prince" are stockier versions. The "Churchwarden" with its stem of at least double the normal length, is a classic reading-pipe. Its relatively small bowl has a hollow in the underpart which gives an even, cool smoke.

Further basic types are differentiated according to the stem, which can be particularly long ("Lavot") or rhomboid ("Bulldog"). Facetted bowls provide another basic type. The most well-known of the pipes with a bent stem is the "Prince of Wales". In another type the mouthpiece attaches directly into the stem, the fragile end of which is protected by a metal ring.

In 1890 the firm of Peterson, founded in 1875 in Dublin, developed a cooling system which, despite its age, is by no means antiquated. A hole bored in the stem allows the smoke to cool off and become milder. The present-day firm of Kapp & Peterson Ltd have 60 different models on offer. The flat mouthpieces direct the smoke upwards. Peterson pipes are particularly popular among those who want a mild smoke. As far as their design is concerned, these Irish models are the direct equivalents of English models. For several decades the firm has concentrated on producing well-tried classical models in unchanged form.

Another English firm, Charatan, specializes in oversize pipes, the well-made "Giants". A further ten or so pipe-makers in Great Britain are known on the continent and overseas.

French pipes from the firm of Butz-Choquin in the traditional pipe-making town of Saint-Claude carry the initials "BC". The firm produces models similar, in their dignified, conservative form, to English ones. Another reputed French firm is Jeantet, which played an important part in the development of practical models such as robust, leather-encased ones for travellers.

The oldest pipe-maker in the Federal Republic of Germany is Vauen-AG in Nuremberg, founded in 1848. At the turn of the century, Vauen started selling pipe-filters made of absorbent paper with an active charcoal element which had been patented by a Dr. Perl. Such filter elements are standard features of Vauen pipes, which are distinguished by a white spot on their mouthpieces which is rather larger than the Dunhill trademark. Probably both marks developed independently of each other.

Coloured spots are, indeed, a favourite sign of quality among pipe-makers. Export models from Vauen carry a blue or a grey spot. Howal pipes from the German Democratic Republic have a red or a gold spot.

One feature of pipes from the Federal Republic of Germany is the use of new materials which have been tried and tested in other areas of industry. Black acrylic glass is used to give mouth pieces a permanent polish. Pyrolitic and Pyroceram, fire-retarding materials developed in the aerospace industry, provide linings for briar pipes, so that these no longer have to be broken in over a long period.

The first Danish pipe-maker chose an English name for commercial reasons: "Stanwell". However, Danish, and Scandinavian pipes in general, have now gained an international reputation of their own for quality. The typical *Danske pibe* produced since the Second World War is hand-finished. Small family firms often produced no more than a few hundred pipes per year.

W.Ø.Larsen was one of the leading creators of such "freehand" pipes. Like Alfred Dunhill, Larsen began his career selling tobacco. The elegant building in the old city of Copenhagen which houses, in addition to the tobacco shop, a comprehensive collection of pipes, points to Larsen having been a supplier to the royal court. And the prices of his creations are suitably royal as well: 500 to 1000 kroner.

Another Danish master is Jens Chonowitsch, whose excellent products are often only available after a long waiting period—only forty or so are produced each month. Asari, a Japanese artist, used a study-visit to Chonowitsch to learn the gentle art, and now products by "Asari Tokyo" are first-class pipes distinguished by the complicated forms given to the bowls.

Jörn Mikke, one of the best-known Danish designers, used Nordic gods as inspiration for his superb Valhalla Collection. A red and white spot is the trademark of the only female pipe-maker, Anne Julie, who took over the business when her husband died.

In addition to the unique creations of the freehand makers, mass-produced models in the modern Scandinavian style are made by various firms. Among these are Stanwell pipes, which carry a solid silver "S" with a crown as well as some 100,000 pipes produced annually by the Jensen firm.

Producers outside Denmark have also adapted to the fashion. Traditional forms and well-proportioned modern creations appear in roughly equal numbers. If models are too extreme in their design they do not go down well among pipe-smokers, who are, on the whole, conservative.

Among the eastern European countries, Czechoslovakia is one of the leaders in the production of briar pipes. Pipes from Proseč are bought by costumers in 35 countries in four continents. The Soviet pipe-carver Fedorov from Leningrad became known internationally for his "Maigret" pipe, which he created for the Belgian thriller-writer and creator of Inspector Maigret, Georges Simenon.

Briar pipes will probably continue to dominate the market. Plastic pipes in pop colours or with artificial grain, which can be bought in the USA, have failed to catch on. Though such plastic pipes can compete with briar pipes as far as smoking quality, weight and hygiene are concerned, smokers prefer wood, because it is more personal and alive. This does not mean that new materials have no future at all. In the 1970s, a light weight metal pipe became a favourite. The "Falcon" model, with an exposed smoke-channel inside an open stem has become popular with smokers looking for a light, easily-looked-after pipe.

Parallel to the development of the various cooling systems for pipes, the tobacco industry has brought out mild tobacco blends to meet the taste of modern smokers. There is smoky, aromatic Lakatia tobacco from Syria, light-coloured, dry Dutch blends and various sorts flavoured with rum, whisky, Irish coffee, honey, aniseed or plums. The production of pipe-tobacco, vacuum-packed, in airtight tins or in practical pouches, has become a major industry. Given the huge variety of carefully blended mixtures, it is no longer necessary to mix one's own. If tobacco shops nevertheless produce personal blends for their customers and keep these in supply with personalized identification numbers, then this is just another aspect of the ritual and mystique surrounding pipe-smoking. In many countries, including the two German states, tax-regulations do not permit such practices.

Smokers with sensitive taste-buds prefer Cavendish mixtures, in which the tobacco is subjected to pressure and heat and undergoes a second fermentation which releases a full aroma even at lower burning temperatures.

For pipes with small bore bowls finely shredded, strong "shag" is best. Sherlock Holmes' partner, Dr. Watson, once received the following instructions:

"When you pass Bradley's would you ask him to send up a pound of the strongest shag tobacco?... My first impression as I opened the door was that a fire had broken out, for the room was so filled with smoke that the light of the lamp upon the table was blurred by it. As I entered, however, my fears were set at rest, for it was the acrid fumes of strong, coarse tobacco which took me by the throat and set me coughing."

The oil millionaire, Henry Deterding only smoked cheap sailors' tobacco. Josef Stalin used to fill his pipe with tobacco taken out of cigarettes of the brand "Herzegovina Flor".

The pipe, which in its porcelain era had been a mark of social position, has become, in the briar era, a status-symbol. Writers, academics and politicians like to be seen with their pipe; the pose of the relaxed smoker suggests they have a similarly relaxed approach to their jobs.

The industry devotes much time and money to advertising smokers' utensils. There are special gas lighters where the flame emerges at an angle, pipe-cases with complete collections including all the accessories, special cork devices for knocking the ash out of pipes with especially fragile bowls.

Even the early wooden pipes were used for caricaturing individuals, and briar pipes can also be given human forms. There are pipes with accurate portraits of Erich Ollenhauer and John F. Kennedy. Often such pipes border on kitsch, as when they have the form of a football boot and football, or a toilet complete with seat (as illustrated in the catalogue of an American firm). But the height of absurdity was reached in some of the creations of the old master, Dunhill—ranging from umbrellas for pipes to the briar pipes which appeared some years ago decorated with finely painted but completely inappropriate far-eastern enamel miniatures.

Cigars

It was the Hamburg merchant, Schlottmann, who discovered the cigar in Spain. It appealed to him, and he had the method of its production explained to him in detail. In 1788 he started to produce cigars himself in Hamburg. Initially they did not sell well, probably because the price was well above that of pipe-tobacco.

In 1809 the first edition of the Brockhaus Conversation Lexicon expressed itself cautiously about the cigar: "A particular method of smoking tobacco should be mentioned here, namely the cigarros: these are leaves which are rolled together to form hollow cylinders of about the thickness of a finger, are then lit at one end and smoked by inserting the other end in the mouth. This method of smoking, which is used instead of a pipe in Spanish America, is beginning to be common in our country; whether it results in an enhanced enjoyment of the tobacco, or not, is difficult to determine."

In 1813 the owner of a tobacco shop in Stans (Austria) had a sign painted which, in addition to the double eagle, two bundles of tobacco and a pipe-smoker, also showed a packet of cigars. Gradually cigar-smoking spread. The cigar was popular because it was easier to smoke, not involving the same amount of preparation as a pipe. Soon on trains—the new method of travelling—one only saw members of the lower classes smoking pipes; the fashion-conscious gentleman puffed on a cigar.

In 1831, when Asian flu first created terror in central Europe, a number of precautionary regulations were issued. One of these was that tobacco smoke protected one from infection. In Berlin the ban on smoking in public was temporarily lifted. In addition to tobacconists, grocers started selling cigars. The Berlin merchant, Buddee, hit on the idea of offering his customers a glass cigar-holder with his cigars. Street merchants sold their wares from trays in garden restaurants. Their characteristic cries of *"Cigarro avec du feu!"* could be heard from afar.

Soon pipes were regarded as philistine by the dandies of the time. They were smoked at home—in public, one was seen smoking a casual cigar. During the Restoration, conservatives regarded cigar-smoking as revolutionary, with its overtones of democratic levelling-down of social customs. Thus the reactionary *Neue preussische Staatszeitung* (New Prussian State Newspaper) complained: "The cigar is the height of casualness. A young person with a cigar in his mouth dares to say and do entirely different things to what he would say and do without a cigar."

Bremen, which after Amsterdam was the most important centre of the cigar industry, hastened the arrival of cheap cigars for all by the introduction of machines into the production process. Quality cigars, however, are carefully handmade to this day. While wine-buffs prefer the purest wines where possible, in the case of cigars it is the blending of up to ten different sorts of tobacco which produces the desired effects. Every cigar consists of three elements: "filler", "binder" and "wrapper". The maker selects a suitable proportion of filling, forms the necessary shape, rolls a leaf round it (the "binder") and presses this into a wooden mould. Twenty rolls are put in a mould at a time. They are regularly turned so that no edges are produced by the pressure. Care has to be taken even at this stage to ensure that the cigar should burn evenly. The pressed roll is taken over by another worker who gives the cigar its

84 Kukryniksy (Kupriyanov, Krylov, Sokolov), caricature of the pipe-smoker Ilya Ehrenburg, 1927

outward form. Using a special knife he separates half a tobacco leaf (the "wrapper") from the main rib and wraps the roll in this. According to which part of the leaf is used, a distinction is made between right-rolled and left-rolled cigars. Left-rolled ones have the lighter underside of the leaf on the outside; protruding veins can affect the look of the cigar. Tobacco powder is used to give the cigar an even colour.

The finished cigars are then sorted according to colour. American producers have a presorter who divides the cigars into broad categories: grey, fawn, blond, brown, red, before they are subdivided into anything up to 180 finely differentiated colours. Such fine distinctions make great demands on the eyesight of the sorters and have no significance as far as quality is concerned. The Bremen method is to pre-sort into light, medium and dark, and then to differentiate between red, brown, and light fawn. In Hamburg, five to six colours are differentiated. The sorter arranges the cigars in the boxes according to colour. Particular care is accorded to the final, top layer.

It is usual to pack cigars in boxes of 10, 20, 50 or 100. Modern methods of packing with cellophane or tin are practical and hygienic, but according to the connoisseurs do not let the tobacco breathe. For good cigars the firms themselves produce boxes made of pleasantly aromatic Gabun wood (okoume), cedar (*Cedrela odorata*) or finished indigenous wood.

The lid, sides and fastening of the wooden boxes are decorated with pictures and advertisements. By the end of the 19th century these had become characterized by excessive richness, sickly sentimentalism and nationalistic arrogance. Obscure medallions from trade exhibitions were supposed to suggest high quality. A few firms avoided such misuse of graphic art and continued to show traditional bird's-

eye views of their factories or other scenes. Only Havana cigars have always been sold in boxes decorated simply with their trademark, the exclusivity of such cigars requiring no more explicit advertisement. Since about 1890, particularly exquisite cigars have been sold separately in polished glass tubes, in wooden boxes with sliding lids for one cigar only or in aroma-sealed aluminium receptacles. 101

With the introduction of cigar bands, in about 1900, a whole new hobby for enthusiastic collectors came into being. The inventor of these decorative bands is supposed to have been Gustav Block, a planter in Cuba. Originally the cigar bands only denoted the trade-name of the cigar. But today collectors can find ones with historical buildings, city coats of arms, folk-costumes, to mention the most popular. In the Soviet Union, a series with portraits of famous clowns was issued. Emil Sierotta, a Berlin collector, has in his collection over 10,000 bands from eleven countries. 102 111,112

After 1900, these cigar bands were collected above all by women and girls. It was regarded as "modern" to stick them on glass mats, ash

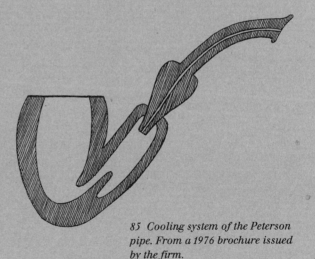

85 Cooling system of the Peterson pipe. From a 1976 brochure issued by the firm.

trays and glasses. There were even instruction booklets on how to create such "mosaics".

Even for non-smokers, Havana cigars are the epitome of highest quality. However, the Havana cigars available in Europe are very different from the genuine Cuban ones produced in the growing-areas measuring about 30 by 120 kilometres round the capital, Havana. Cuban tobacco is largely only used for the initial covering, the final covering usually being lighter-coloured, either Indonesian or local European tobacco. The same applies to Brazilian cigars.

Over the last hundred years the taste of European cigar smokers has changed considerably. Honoré de Balzac, himself a cigar-smoker, wrote: "O now to smoke . . . to see how a Havana cigar, two fingers thick, burns in front of my lips, wraps me in pleasant dreams, dissolves into blue smoke—like love." It was the narcotic effect of the strong tobacco, referred to here by Balzac, which led a later generation of smokers to prefer the more stimulating effects of a lighter cigar, or the smaller cigarillo.

The trade jargon of the cigar industry has largely come from the countries of Latin America—proof of their earlier predominance in the market. Classical forms are the torpedo-shaped, pointed "Regalia" and the shorter "Trabucco". The "Stumpen", open at the end to be lit, is a Swiss invention which is largely machine-made. In 1847 in Ticino the light "Virginia" with a long mouthpiece was invented.

Originally, cigar shops bought their wares in large cases of 1000 cigars. Rich smokers bought similar supplies, which they stored in their wine cellars. For one's daily needs there were simple wooden boxes, decorative containers for one's desk or even containers in the shape of books bearing the title *Collected Works of Dr. Smoke.*

In 1842 Girandet invented the leather cigar pouch with steel reinforcements. A year later, Prützmann perfected it with the addition of partitions which enabled cigars to be carefully carried separately from each other. Modern tobacco boxes for cigars are equipped with humidity regulators, thermometers and hygrometers.

The traditional meerschaum centres produced cigar-holders from this material using methods which hardly differed from those used for pipes. As no protective layer of soot forms in cigar-smoking, these holders had to be given a carefully inserted lining.

Louis II of Bavaria had a replica of the state carriage with six horses carved on a meerschaum cigar-holder 56 centimetres long and 20 centimetres high, which he then gave to a court actor. He himself possessed a holder of similar design made of ivory.

The Austrian emperor, Francis Joseph, was presented with a modernistic electric cigar-lighter by the German Kaiser William II. Today it can be found in the museum which is housed in his residence in Linz.

Among keen smokers of cigars were Richard Wagner, Mark Twain, Georges Bizet, Winston Churchill and the former UN General Secretary, U Thant. Johannes Brahms smoked such strong cigars that his friends said one could only gain pleasure from smoking half of one at the most.

In the countries of Latin America and in Spain and Portugal cigar-smoking women were by no means a rare sight. In central Europe this was not the case, where cigar-smoking women were not nearly as common as women smoking pipes.

In the Focke-Museum in Bremen one can see a reconstruction of C. Friese's tobacco shop as it was in 1860. In Turku (Finland) there is a replica of a tobacco shop from the last century. *104*

Cigarettes

Round about 1720 the snuff-manufacturers in Seville also started to produce cigarettes, which were called "papelitos" or "pagitas". Giacomo Casanova, whose memoirs, in addition to the erotic adventures they recount, furnish us with many interesting insights into life in the 18th century, described a Spanish publican who smoked cigarettes: "The good man carelessly smoked his cigarito of Brazilian tobacco in a rolled-up piece of paper, puffing out thick clouds of smoke in a self-important manner."

Georges Bizet has immortalized the Spanish cigarette girls in his opera *Carmen*. The chorus of girls sings:

Smoke flies like a lover's sighs,
rising, gently rising up to the sky
and is lost in heaven's glory,
but the smoke in lovers' eyes
can be blinding

From Spain, cigarettes spread to other countries. In France they were manufactured from 1844 onwards. At first heavy American tobaccos were used which after a couple of puffs had a narcotic effect on the senses and did not give a consistent smoke. It was only when lighter oriental tobaccos started to be used that the cigarette became at all widespread. Climatic conditions allow tobacco to mature properly in Anatolia, Greece, Italy, and Bulgaria. Undesirable protein compounds do not have to be removed by a complicated fermentation process, but disappear as the crop ripens.

The light oriental cigarette began its triumphant march through Europe from Russia in the middle of the 19th century. During the Crimean War in 1856 the British, French and Italians came to like the light cigarettes which one could roll oneself and which did not have to be kept in any special conditions. Returning soldiers helped spread the new smoking fashion in their respective countries, making them popular in their clubs and persuading local tobacconists to stock them.

In 1862 a Russian set up the first German cigarette factory in Dresden. In 1909 in the same city the eccentric building housing the cigarette firm of Yenidze was constructed. The architect Martin Hammitsch designed a domed building reminiscent of an oriental mosque with bright tiled exterior and a chimney disguised as a minaret. The factory was one of the first buildings in Europe to be constructed on the framework principle. The name of the factory was derived from an important tobacco-growing area of Turkey. Today this imaginative building is a warehouse for the state tobacco company Tabakkontor.

The cigarette, at first derided as a replacement for stronger forms of tobacco for those who were weak of constitution, took over as the leading form of tobacco by the outbreak of the First World War—a position which it has retained ever since. Oscar Wilde praised the cigarette as follows: "The cigarette is the perfect expression of a perfect pleasure. It is exquisite yet fails to satisfy us. What more can one desire." Produced for mass consumption, intended for a short, intensive moment of pleasure, the cigarette is, at the most elegant, never precious.

It is only by fully automated production methods that the required quantities of cigarettes can be produced. The monthly production of individual firms is measured in millions.

In 1878 the Frenchman Durand demonstrated his cigarette machine at the Paris World Exhibition. Two years later Bergstössner in Russia showed a further development, which was taken up by the American Bonsack and was introduced into factories. After 1910, the cigarette makers were everywhere ousted by machines.

The production process involves the mixing of several sorts of tobacco; thus small—climatically caused—fluctuations in individual harvests can be overcome. Mixing is followed by cutting and filling. Even at the turn of the century, Bonsack machines were producing 50,000 to 60,000 cigarettes per day. Modern Swedish machines can produce a million daily. The paper cover is given the appropriate trademark before packing.

In recent years there has been an increase in the proportion of filter cigarettes sold, and also the proportion of cigarettes which are claimed to be "low tar". Originally a cork fulfilled the function of a filter.

After the Second World War, when the allies occupied Germany, cigarettes attained the status of black market currency. It was mainly heavy American makes which were smoked. In the 1950s lighter cigarettes came onto the market, and now account for 80 per cent of total consumption. In 1968 the cigarette industry in the Federal Republic of Germany was producing 7,900 million cigarettes per month, of which only 1,000 million were without filter. And this trend towards lighter brands is a world-wide one. Even in France, where the strong "Gauloise" is almost a part of the nation's image, the market share of low-tar cigarettes has risen by 10 per cent in a few years.

There are different factors which account for the increase in the numbers of mild filter cigarettes being smoked. On the one hand there has simply been a change in public taste, on the other hand, the influence of medical campaigns should not be underestimated.

For a long time the war against smoking was waged largely by certain groups which rejected all forms of tobacco on religious, political or health grounds. Before the First World War young anarchists used to sing:

O holy Fridolin, holy Fridolin,
let bourgeois lungs gasp with nicotine,
we anarchists are here again!

In many countries associations of anti-smokers were formed. As the arguments of those opposed to tobacco did not differentiate between use and abuse, their attempts met only little success. It was not until a more discerning medical campaign—which now even exists at UN level—was started that any success was achieved.

Further support for mild cigarettes came from the increased number of female smokers. Hitherto women had only competed with men in snuff-taking. Women smoking pipes or cigars were regarded as regional peculiarities or early fighters for emancipation.

For about fifty years the industry has been producing aromatic cigarettes for women. Propolis, a sticky wax produced by bees, was one of the earliest aromatic substances used for this purpose. In the thirties in Britain, special smoking compartments for women were introduced by the London and North-Western Railway.

Advertising plays an important role in the cigarette industry. Cleverly designed packets, king-size formats and gold effects are used by advertising psychologists to make up for the lack of qualitative differences between individual brands. Hans Neuerburg, one of the five biggest cigarette companies in the Federal Republic budgetted 4 to 5 million marks for advertising in 1960.

PIPES WITH COOLING SYSTEMS

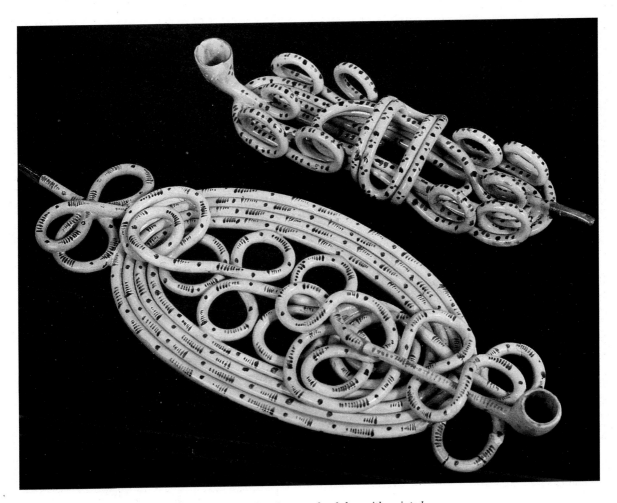

86 Two snake pipes made of clay with painted
decoration. Staffordshire, around 1780, lengths 36
and 24 cm. Syring Collection

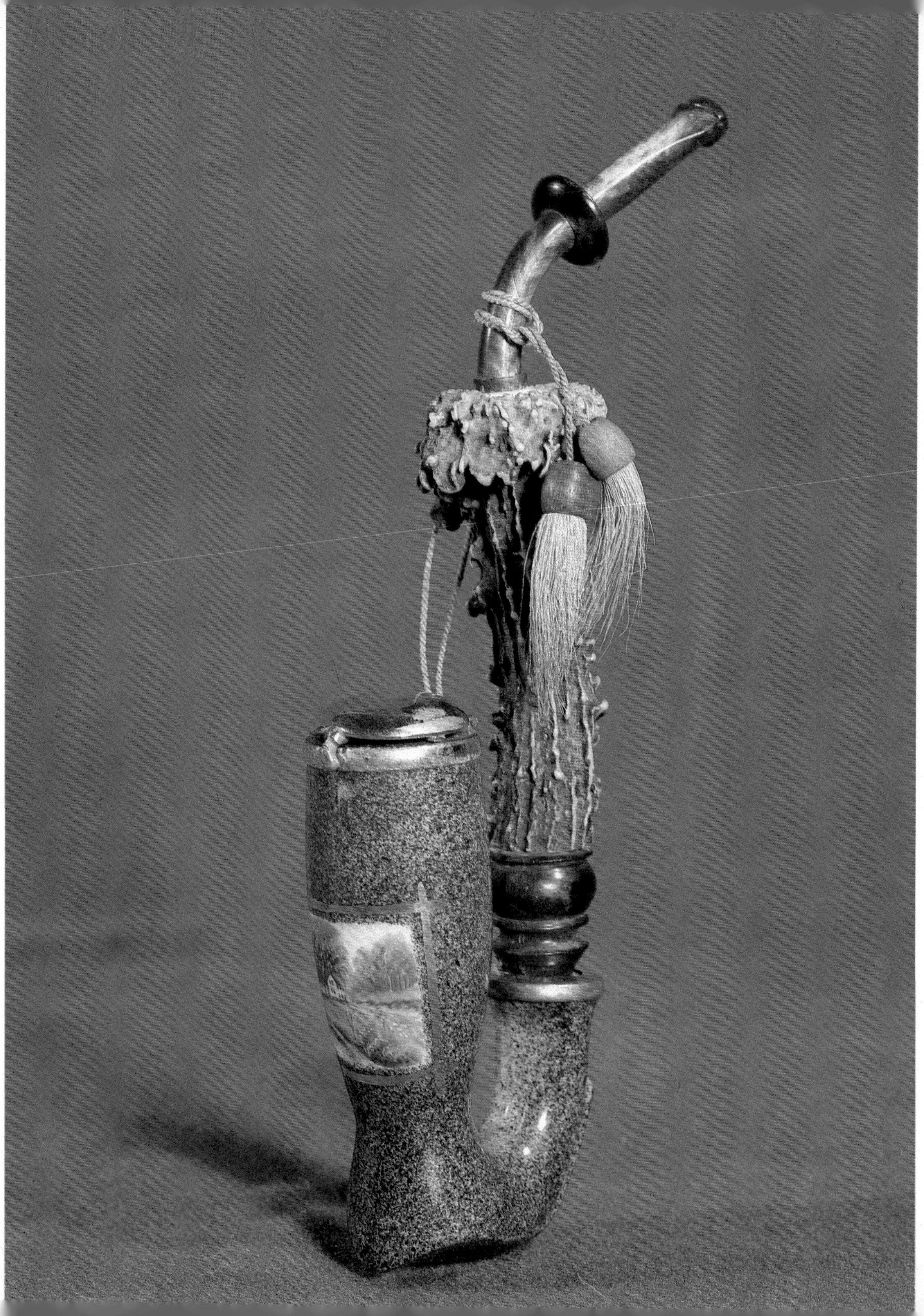

87 *Two-sectioned pipe made of stone-glass and antler horn. On the bowl a depiction of a landscape. Early 19th century, height 11 cm. Museum für Deutsche Geschichte, Berlin*

88 *Brass pipe-bowl with heraldic relief, lid in form of a kettle. 19th century, height 9.5 cm. Museum für Deutsche Geschichte, Berlin*

89 Pipe-bowl made of polished granite. Mid-19th century, height 8.2 cm. Historisches Museum, Schwerin

*90 Wooden pipe-bowl with tin appliqué.
Arkhangelsk, 19th century, height 16 cm.
Museum für Völkerkunde, Leipzig*

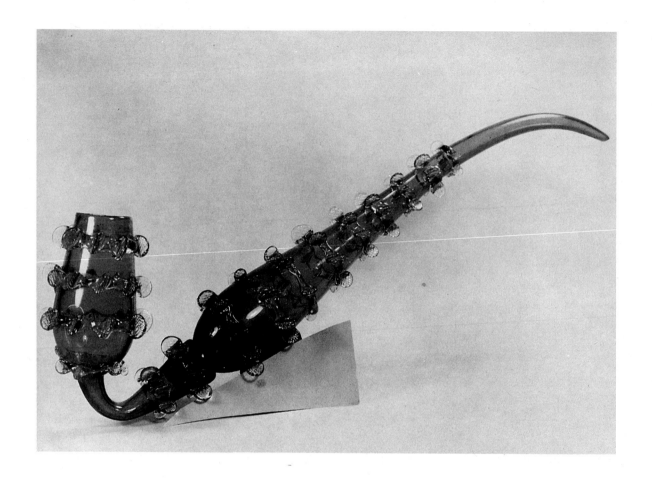

92 Goral pipe made of softwood with brass covering. High Tatra, Poland, acquired 1974, length 21 cm. Libert Collection

93 Wooden pipe covered with silver plate. Early 20th century, length 22 cm. Libert Collection

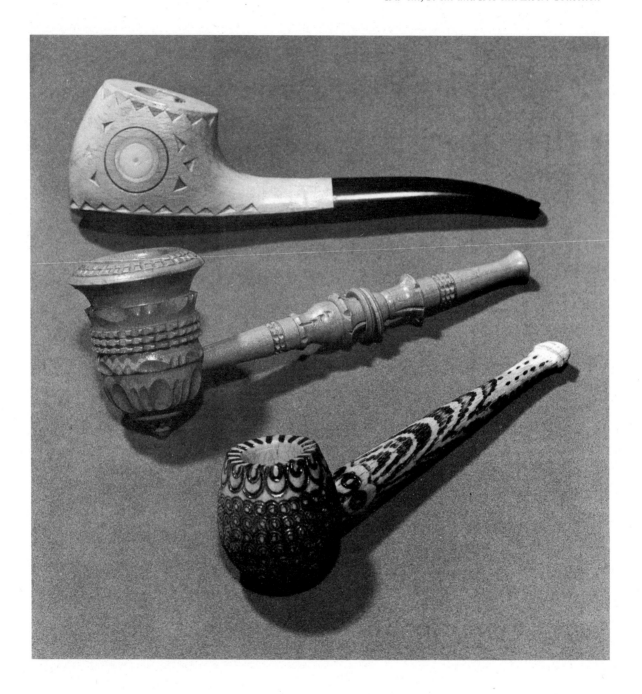

BRIAR PIPES

*95 Contemporary freehand-made briar pipe from
Denmark, length 16.5 cm. Archiv Danske Pibe, Hamburg*

96–98 *Modern freehand-made pipes, briar, Denmark,*
length 14.8 cm, length 16.8 cm and height of bowl 5 cm.
Archiv Danske Pibe, Hamburg

99 *Italian briar pipe. Pipes made of this particularly light-coloured wood appear on the market under the name of "sea coral". Height of bowl 5.5 cm. Archives of the Savinelli firm, Milan*

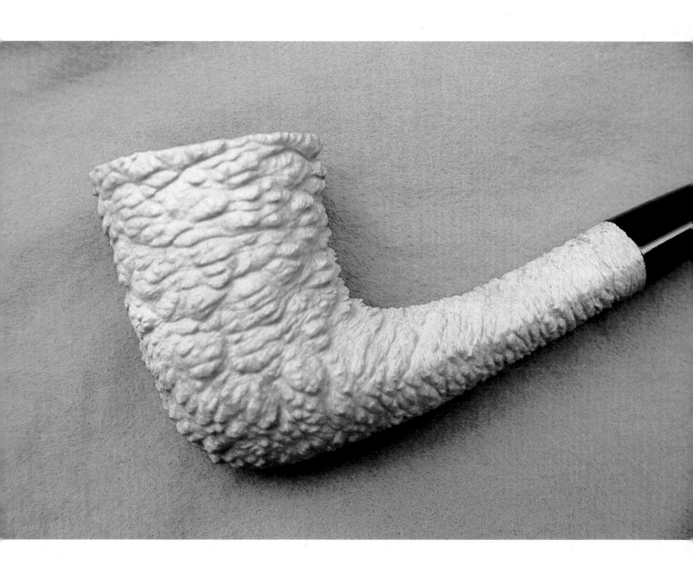

100 Corn-cob pipe, marketed as "Missouri meer-schaum". The plastic mouthpiece contains a paper filter. Washington, Missouri, length 18 cm. Libert Collection

In 1898 Alfons Maria Mucha from Prague created a six-colour advertisement for cigarette paper of the "JOB" brand. Overprinted colours lend the poster an iridescent quality. Mucha's golden-haired advertisement girl constitutes one of the high points of art nouveau graphic art.

114

Cigarettes are meant for instant, transitory pleasure and therefore do not have much concomitant paraphernalia. Outward appearances were more important than actual value. Typical objects are the art deco cases in alpaca (plated German silver) with delightful inset decorations in plastic. Cigarette holders of

101 *Cigar shop in Bremen harbour area. Steel engraving by H. W. Brennhäuser after a painting by H. Romberg:*
Die feinste Sorte *(The finest type). Mid-19th century.*
Focke-Museum, Bremen

102 *Cigar band, Netherlands. Libert Collection*

exaggerated length were popular. Edgar Wallace, the successful detective writer, had his photograph taken with one of these holders.

By analogy with the pipe-tamper in the shape of a woman's leg, porcelain manufacturers produced similar cigarette holders. Carved holders produced by folk-artists were relatively rare. The most likely carvers of such objects, the shepherds and foresters only came to the cigarette relatively late, if at all.

And these professions were being subjected to changes which led to the death of the tradition of carving.

High-class accessories were made in the pioneer country of the modern cigarette industry, Russia. As early as the 1840s the porcelain manufacturers in St. Petersburg produced a service with twelve pipe-shaped cigarette-holders. In the Ivanovo area a sizeable lacquered goods industry developed in the 17th century. Peasants painted miniatures in the winter months as an extra source of income. Papier-mâché and wooden objects were painted with a lacquer based on egg-tempera and vinegar.

Since the 1920s and 1930s this folk-art has undergone a revival in the Soviet Union. Cigarette cases in the Ivanovo State Museum demonstrate the consummate skill of these Russian folk-artists, who derived their inspiration from the rich folk-poetry of their culture. Popular motifs on these black cases are galloping troikas, knights on horseback and scenes which suggest that the finished objects were used as gifts for lovers.

In the Balkans there was a popular belief that the way an individual smoked a cigarette revealed much about that person's character. Someone who gazed thoughtfully at the cloud of smoke was a lovable fool, someone who exhaled the smoke rapidly through his nose was aggressive and someone who smoked his cigarette evenly could be trusted.

Chewing-tobacco

In certain jobs smoking is not possible because of the fire risk. In addition to this, all forms of smoking involve certain regular hand-movements. Because of this, miners, mill-workers and seamen use chewing-tobacco as an alternative.

The term "chewing-tobacco" is a misnomer, for the wad of tobacco is not chewed but rather inserted between the cheek and the jaw and sucked.

Originally hanks of smoking-tobacco were probably used. Genuine chewing-tobacco exist-ed in Sweden as early as 1680. In Germany and the Netherlands, production started in around 1800. The compact wad of tobacco was called a *pruim* (plum) in Low German. Production cen-tres grew up in Flensburg, Kiel and Nordhausen. Heavy American tobacco was used which had a high nicotine content of about 4.5 per cent. The tobacco was packed in barrels in New Orleans and transported by sailing ships to Europe—a journey of 90 days, during which the leaves fer-mented. However, the long journey increased the price considerably, and therefore Nordhau-sen, after the world economic crisis of 1929, started to import considerably cheaper Ken-tucky tobacco, which was cultivated in Italy for cigarette manufacture.

After harvesting, the leaves were smoked over open hardwood fires. Then each half of the leaf was immersed in a warm wash, the ingre-dients of which—precise details were a closely guarded secret in each firm—remind one of a recipe for some sort of spiced cake: honey, glu-cose, fruit juices, cloves (*Syzygium aromati-cum*), cinnamon (*Cinnamomum verum*), ani-seed (*Pimpinella anisum*), licorice. The final flavouring was completed with the addition of strong red wine, rum or sherry. The mixture was allowed to mature for several days in oak casks. Then the tobacco, with its covering leaves, was twisted into a long rope which was then rolled up and put in a drying room. Finally *119* the covering leaves were further flavoured with syrup or fruit extracts and had preserva-tives added (glycerine, salts, tannic acid). Orig-inally the customer bought a skein of tobacco and cut off lengths for himself. Nowadays, prac- *118* tical ready-for-use pieces are sold in tins or packed in cellophane.

Tobacco is chewed as a stimulant by those in-volved in heavy manual labour. Its use merely for pleasure is secondary. Therefore the con-tainers used for it were seldom decorated to

103 *Carved cigarette-holder. Germany, 20th century, length 12 cm. Stadtmuseum, Schwedt (Oder)*

120 any great extent. Only in the case of seamen did their hobby of wood-carving include containers for chewing-tobacco.

The larger firms used grey-blue glazed stoneware pots with two knob-shaped handles as advertisements for their chewing-tobacco. 19th-century pots of this type originating from the Nordhausen firm of Hannewacker or from *115* Joseph Doms of Ratibor (Racibórz, Poland) can often be found decorating the shelves of old inns.

The German writer, Kurt Tucholsky, wrote about such tobacco in a poem which immortalized another firm. The refrain goes:

Chewing baccy, chewing baccy,
a little wad of chewing baccy,
from the firm of Eckenbrecht
in Kiel.

In Europe, the chewing of tobacco was restricted to certain occupations, whereas in the USA it was more widespread. Charles Dickens, who travelled in the States in 1842, called Washington the "capital of tobacco spitting". Even in public buildings spitting tobacco juice was quite normal, the novelist noted with some distaste in his travel memoirs. In recent years, chewing-tobacco with a light, almost sweet taste has come to Europe from the USA and has become increasingly popular. Chewers of tobacco are in good company—many famous people have indulged in the pastime—the best known being Lord Nelson.

Curiosities, clubs, records

The history of tobacco recounted so far has already included a number of curious developments. But there were others which arose purely out of the desire to be original or to set up records.

One special category includes smokers' accessories which are combined with other kinds of objects. One early example of such multi-use objects was the snuff-box owned by the cavalry General von Ziethen, which was part of his *18* walking-stick. Such sticks were, up till the turn of the century an integral part of outdoor clothing, and combinations with other objects were therefore common. As far as the history of smoking is concerned, pipe-cases, cigar-containers, cigarette-tampers and cigar-lighters all as part of hollow sticks are worth mentioning.

The combining of tobacco pipe and weapon has also been known since the 18th century. Indian chiefs received from French traders war-axes whose hollow handles served as mouthpieces. The pipe-bowl was screwed on above the blade. This European invention became very popular among the Red Indians. French and English traders bartered large numbers of such "tomahawk-pipes" for furs.

An American inventor constructed a pipe-pistol, which only looked outwardly like a pipe, and named it "cool smoke". In his book, *Firearms curiosa*, Winant mentions another variant of this type of pistol which he claims could actually also be used as a pipe.

The Tobacco Museum in Bünde, Westphalia (Federal Republic of Germany), holds the record for the largest-known pipe—a wooden giant weighing almost 175 kilogrammes. In

1937, responding to an American attempt to set up a record, cigar-makers in Bünde produced a giant cigar 1.65 metres long. In 1981 this record was beaten by a cigar produced in Las Palmas and auctioned in London which was 3.8 metres long and weighed 110 kilos. In Andorra, enormous cigars almost 1 metre long are displayed in popular processions.

An object without much practical use was the cigar-seesaw which received an Imperial German Patent No. 81,413; its seesaw movement was supposed to ensure that a cigar burnt evenly when not in use. Advertised as "the most senseless apparatus in the world" by the very Nuremberg firm that made it; the "Aaatchoo snuff-machine" had a lever on a spring which flicked the snuff into one's nose.

The manufacture of cigarettes started in Austria in 1865. First, "double cigarettes", three times the normal length, were produced, which had a mouthpiece on each side and were separated before use.

104 *Cutting of the wad. Detail from an emergency currency note. Nordhausen, Harz, 1920. Libert Collection*

Smokers desiring a civilized atmosphere in which to indulge themselves founded clubs in many countries, in which social events, talks and competitions were organized. In Germany during the period 1878–1890, when all social-democratic activities were banned, some of

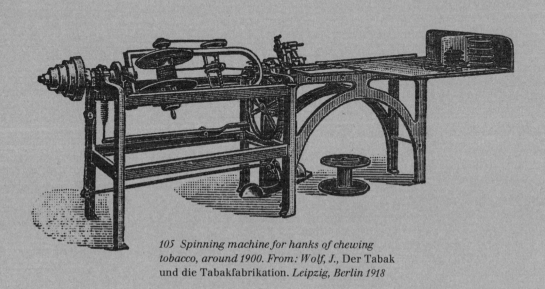

105 *Spinning machine for hanks of chewing tobacco, around 1900. From:* Wolf, J., Der Tabak und die Tabakfabrikation. *Leipzig, Berlin 1918*

these pipe-smokers' clubs took on political significance. Under cover of such legal foundations the workers were able to continue their attempts to organize themselves. In 1879 the pipe-smokers' club in Dittersdorf, near Zwickau, was banned by the police on the grounds that its members were indulging in illegal social-democratic activities. During this period of anti-socialist legislation the smokers' clubs played a role which has hitherto been largely ignored and is worthy of investigation.

Smokers' clubs which still exist have, as their central objective, the aesthetic enjoyment of tobacco—the best way of achieving this, and the highest form of smoking, being pipe-smoking. These clubs arrange tobacco-sampling sessions, exchanges with other clubs and smoking competitions.

In the constitution of the Scandinavian "Nordisk Tobakskollegium", paragraph 2 lays down that members should smoke their tobacco "thoughtfully". This club brings together tobacconists, pipe-makers and tobacco-importers, as well as smokers. Excursions to pipe-makers' workshops are even organized. Since 1978 the club has published the journal *Piber & Tobak.*

In various cities there are special clubs for female smokers. One of the most recent of such foundations was in the Polish city of Nova Huta.

In 1928 a 28-year-old woman won second place in a cigar competition organized by the *Deutscher Raucherverband* (German smokers' association). When the same organization held a competition for the title of Berlin Master-Smoker in 1935, members of 71 clubs competed for the first prize of 5 pounds of tobacco. The rules laid down that a short shag pipe filled with 4 grammes of tobacco and lit by a single match was to be used. The *Deutsche Allgemeine Zeitung* published a long article describing the exciting competition: "During the first minute of the competition 'Kornblume I' and half a minute later 'Perle II' threw in the towel. Their representatives' pipes had gone out and relighting was forbidden. What was at stake was: who can go on longest? After three-quarters of an hour 39 competitors were still in the running—and how!

Tensely they looked at their pipes, carefully they drew on them. . . After the 51st minute there were still 24 smokers in the competition. Now the field was clear. They smoked on with utmost concentration, and during the next six minutes not one dropped out. But the final four would not give in. An hour and a quarter had already gone by. Then, after an hour and sixteen minutes the fourth man gave in. Within the next few minutes another two dropped out, leaving only one man. After an hour and $36^{1}/_{2}$ minutes he stood up and said 'Enough's enough'. The 34-year-old had soundly beaten the other competitors—some were over 60 years old (one was even 80!)."

In 1978 a Japanese smoker by the name of Suzuki won the world-championship in slow smoking with 134 minutes for 3 grammes of tobacco. A few months later in Montreux the Italian Vivis Vecchi beat this record by 25 minutes. In doing so he won the 6th European championship against 322 competitors, including 27 women. The last place in the competition was taken by the Swiss Franz Zurwerra, who had to give up after his match broke twice when lighting up.

Other competitions among tobacco-lovers are less spectacular. In 1978 a gentleman by the name of Hutchington won a competition for the most economic cigar-smoking: he smoked his for almost 90 minutes.

About 200 snuff-clubs in the Federal Republic of Germany are concerned, not only with snuff-taking competitions, but also with pre-serving south-German customs.

Chewing-tobacco enthusiasts in the USA regularly hold competitions in distance-spitting. Many local pipe-smokers' clubs in the USA and Canada are members of the International Association of Pipe Smokers' Clubs (I.A.P.S.C.) which has its headquarters in New York.

Hungarian pipe-collectors founded a pipe-enthusiasts' club in the town of Kaposvár. The best-known European clubs are in Finland: Püponplottajat-Valtakunnalinen Piippukerho-jen, Helsinki; France: Pipe-Club de France, Paris; Great Britain: The Pipe Club of Great Britain, London; Italy: Il Club della Pipa, Milan; Scandinavia: Nordisk Tobakskollegium, Roskilde; Switzerland: Pipe Club de Suisse, Lausanne.

Collectors and collections

The first important collections of valuable snuff-boxes were made by feudal rulers. Catherine II, the Russian Tsarina, possessed a large collection which today is one of the treasures in the Hermitage in Leningrad. The sparse remains of the Prussian King Frederick II's collection have already been mentioned. Every now and again snuff-boxes appear on the market which the King had given as presents to favourites or military leaders. In 1954 the auctioneers Sotheby's, in London, auctioned *objets d'art* belonging to the deposed Egyptian King Farouk. Among these were two snuff-boxes originally belonging to Frederick II, which aroused great interest and fetched high prices. In 1982 at an auction in Geneva a box covered with mother-of-pearl and decorated with pre-cious stones, a work of outstanding quality, fetched a record price.

Pipes only rarely achieved the status of being important prestige presents. Napoleon Bonaparte presented victorious generals with pipes decorated with diamonds. Collectors have preserved pipes which were connected with famous people. Included in the memorial museum to Tsar Peter I in the summer-house of the Residence in Leningrad there is an ordinary wooden pipe which the Tsar once smoked. A similar memento, belonging to the Hussar General Lassalle and preserved in the Paris Army Museum, is the meerschaum pipe with which he gave the signal to attack at the battle of Wagram (1809).

Single clay, beechwood and porcelain pipes were often kept for long periods of time by smokers, who clung to such objects—often despite their being clumsily patched—not just out of sentimentality or to save money, but because it is a well-known fact that pipes which have been broken in are more pleasant to smoke than brand new ones. It was not until the introduction of the briar pipe that possession of several pipes became common.

Individual pipe-smokers started to collect various pipes in the 18th century. At the beginning of the 19th century the King of Württemberg and the Duke of Zweibrücken possessed impressive collections. Contemporaries estimated the value of General Vandamme's collection at 60,000 livres. In 1803 Johanna Schopenhauer reported from the Netherlands that many citizens there had their own pipe collections. The Viennese musician Joseph Lanner possessed an excellent collection, the centre-piece of which was a pipe in the shape of an oboe.

Tobacco firms also started collections of smoking paraphernalia and these are accessible to the public either in the firms' own museums or as part of larger collections in regional museums.

Alfred Dunhill, who also published two books about pipes, amassed an important collection which includes the pipe belonging to Sir Walter Raleigh. In the pipe-shop belonging to W.Ø.Larsen in Copenhagen exotic pipes, opium pipes from China and European models can be admired. The most eye-catching exhibit is an enormous meerschaum pipe with motifs from the *Odyssey*.

Pipe-collecting today is by no means the exclusive domain of smokers. An exception, however, must be the Hungarian Lajos Calambas from Kaposvár, who not only collects meerschaum pipes but also carves new ones.

The most important tobacco museums and specialized collections are as follows:

AUSTRIA
Tabakmuseum, Vienna
(Museum of the firm Austria Tabakwerke (AG)
Benediktinerstift Kremsmünster
(snuff-box collection)

BELGIUM
Musée Communal de la Céramique,
Andenne Namur (clay-pipe production)

FEDERAL REPUBLIC OF GERMANY
Deutsches Tabakmuseum, Bünde, Westphalia
Tabakhistorische Sammlung Reemtsma,
Altonaer Museum, Hamburg
Focke-Museum, Bremen
Schnupftabakmuseum Grafenau (snuff)

GERMAN DEMOCRATIC REPUBLIC
Heimatmuseum und Naturalienkabinett,
Waldenburg (sectioned pipes)
Stadtmuseum Schwedt (Oder)
(cigar-production)

Kreisheimatmuseum, Dermbach
(pipe-turner's workshop)

FINLAND
Luistorimäen Käsetyöläismuseo, Turku
(historical tobacconist's shop)

FRANCE
Musée d'intérêt National du Tabac,
Bergerac, Dordogne, Hôtel de Ville
Musée des Pipes, Saint-Claude

GREAT BRITAIN
House of Pipes, Bramber, Sussex
Victoria and Albert Museum, London
(James Collection)
City Museum, Birmingham
(clay-pipe manufacture)

NETHERLANDS
Niemeyer Nederlands Tabacologisch
Museum, Groningen
Pijpen- en Aerdewerkmuseum, Gouda
(clay-pipe manufacture)
Pijpenkamer en Kaffee- en Theekabinett,
Utrecht
(Museum of the firm Douwe Egberts)

POLAND
Museum Chelm
(ethnographic pipe collection)

SWEDEN
Tabakmuseet, Skansen, Stockholm

SWITZERLAND
Musée de la Pipe et des Objets du Tabac,
Lausanne

USA
U.S. Tobaccos Museum, Greenwich,
Connecticut
Metropolitan Museum of Art, New York
(snuff-box collection)

CIGARS

106 Tobacco shop belonging to the Friese firm, Bremen, around 1860. Original interior now in Focke-Museum, Bremen

107 Cigar accessories. The sulphur matches were lit by striking against the ribbed plate. The matches were in one container, a candle in the other. Six cigars could be held in the base plate. The disc under the central cigar cutter was used to knock off the ash. Late 19th century, diameter 21 cm. Stadtmuseum, Schwedt (Oder)

108 Cigar-holder: Leda and the swan. Meerschaum with amber tip, late 19th century, length of head 9.5 cm. Stadtmuseum, Schwedt (Oder)

109 Two-cigar holders in a case. Meerschaum with amber tips, Germany, late 19th century, lengths 12 cm and 13.6 cm. Libert Collection

110 Label on a box of cigars. The excess of gold medals is typical for the period. Germany, around 1900, 16×18 cm. Libert Collection

111 Meerschaum cigar-holder with amber mouthpiece. Around 1900, length 10 cm. Rust Collection

112 Pipe-shaped cigar-holder in the form of a man's head. The individuality of the features suggest that a real person was depicted. Wood with meerschaum inlay, around 1900. Height of head 4 cm. Märkisches Museum, Berlin

113, 114 Cigar bands from Netherlands. Libert Collection

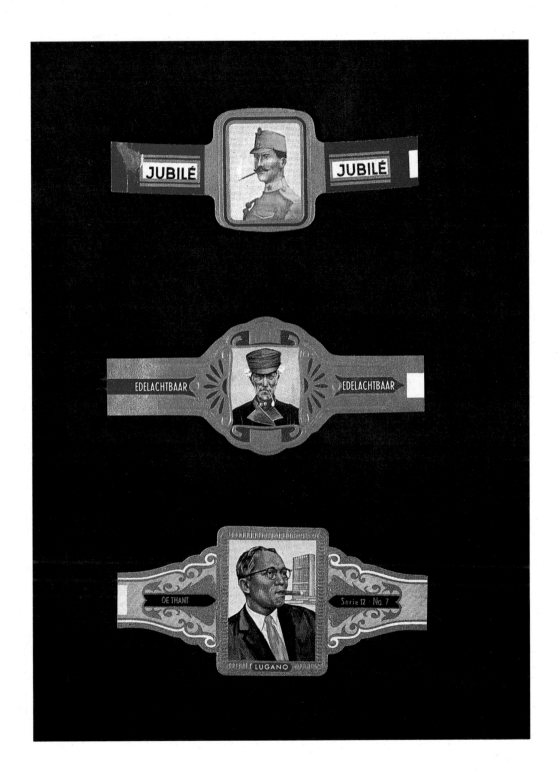

CIGARETTES

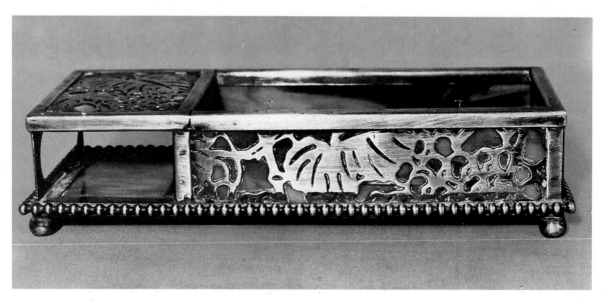

115 *Cigarette-container with match-holder, Tiffany, New York. Filigree work, silver and glass, around 1860, length 14 cm. Museum Viadrina, Frankfurt (Oder)*

116 *Alfons Maria Mucha (1860–1939), advertisement for cigarette paper. Six-colour lithograph, 1898, 51.5×38.5 cm. Städtische Textil- und Kunstgewerbe-sammlung, Karl-Marx-Stadt*

Following pages:

117 *Container for chewing-tobacco made of grey-blue glazed stoneware. Firm of Joseph Doms in Ratibor (Racibórz), Poland, height 18 cm. Stadtmuseum, Schwedt (Oder)*

118 *Porcelain pipe-bowl. Inscription:* Rauch-Club. . . *1886 (Smokers' Club. . . 1886). Probably originated in Berlin, height 10.5 cm. Märkisches Museum, Berlin*

119 *Pipe collection in the Waldenburg Museum, Saxony. The collection dates from the second half of the 19th century and is preserved in its original form.*

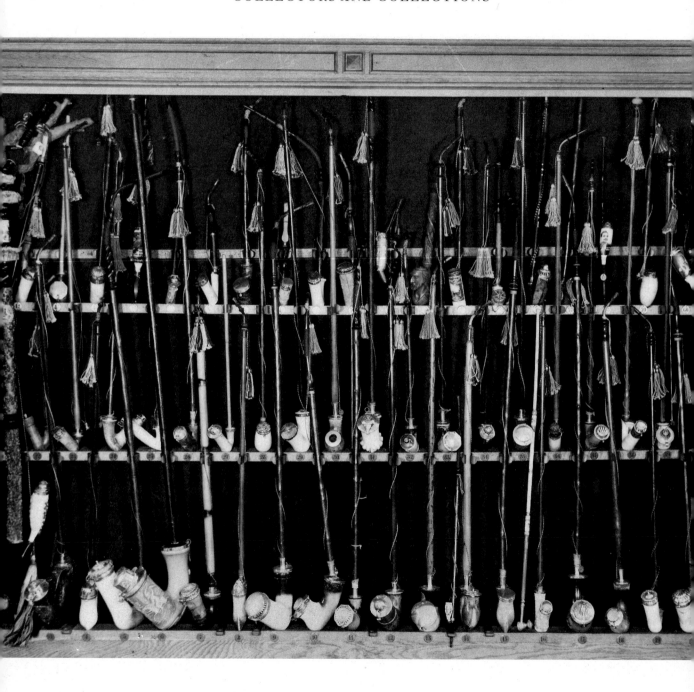

Bibliography

BASTIEN, A.P.: *La pipe.* Paris, 1973.

CONTE CORTI, E.C.: *Die trockene Trunkenheit. Ursprung, Kampf und Triumph des Rauchens.* Leipzig, 1930.

CORBEILLIER, C.DE: *Alte Tabakdosen aus Europa und Amerika.* Munich, no date.

CUDELL, R.: *Das Buch vom Tabak.* Cologne, 1927.

CURTISS, M.M.: *The Book of Snuff and Snuff Boxes.* London, 1935.

DAVIDOFF, Z.: *Das Taschenbuch des Zigarrenrauchers.* Munich, 1982.

DIRK, S.: *Die Cigarette.* Leipzig, 1924.

DUNHILL, A.: *The Pipe Book.* London, 1924.

DUNHILL, A.: *The Gentle Art of Smoking.* London, 1954.

EHRENBURG, I.: *13 Pfeifen.* Berlin, 1930.

FEINHALS, J.: *Der Tabak in Kunst und Kultur.* Cologne, 1926.

FRESCO-CORBU, R.: *European Pipes.* No place of publication, 1982.

Goudsche Pijpen. Amsterdam, 1942.

HARTEL, K.: *Das Taschenbuch vom Schnupftabak.* Munich, 1970.

HOCHRAIN, H.: *Das Taschenbuch des Pfeifenrauchers.* Munich, 1974.

HUGHES, G.B.: *English Snuff Boxes.* London, 1971.

Iserlohner Tabaksdosen. Bilder einer Kriegszeit. Münster, 1982.

LEHMANN, A.H. and ZEIDLER, P.G.: *Blauer Dunst macht Weltgeschichte.* Berlin, 1939.

MARONDE, C.: *Rund um den Tabak.* Frankfurt (Main), 1976.

NEKRASOVA, M.A.: *Palekhaya miniatyura.* Leningrad, 1978.

PRADE, M. DE: *Tabacks-Historia, insonderheit vom Schnupftabak.* Schneeberg, 1747.

PRITTCHETT, R.F.: *Smokiana ethnographical.* No place of publication, 1890.

SCHRANKA, E.M.: *Tabakanekdoten.* Cologne, 1914.

SPRENGLER, P.N.: "Die Tobackspfeifenfabrik", in: *Handwerk und schöne Künste in Tabellen.* Berlin, 1772.

STENGEL, W.: *Tabatieren.* Berlin, 1950.

Tabago. Hamburg, 1960.

Tabakfachbuch. Leipzig, 1953.

Tabaklexikon. Mainz, 1967.

TOMASEK, J.M.: *Die Pfeifen-Industrie.* Weimar, 1878.

VERDAGUER, J.: *Das Pfeifenraucher-Brevier.* Munich, 1980.

WOLF, J.: *Der Tabak und die Tabakfabrikation.* Leipzig, Berlin, 1918.

Index

Numbers in italics refer to the illustrations.

Sources of illustrations

ADN-Zentralbild, Berlin 43
Altonaer Museum, Hamburg 6
Jörg Anders, Berlin (West) 9
Klaus Bergmann, Potsdam 7, 8, 10, 15, 19, 22–25, 36, 37, 41, 44, 45, 56, 57, 60, 61, 63, 68, 70, 71, 72–75, 82, 87, 88, 92, 93, 100, 108, 109, 111, 113, 114
Bundesdenkmalamt, Vienna 12, 13
Titus Czerski, Bremen 48
Danske Pibe Frickert & Behrends, Hamburg 95–98
Walter Danz, Halle 26
Focke-Museum, Bremen 101
Joachim Fritz, Basdorf 5, 47, 117
Germanisches Nationalmuseum, Nuremberg 53
Bernd Giesa, Schwedt (Oder) 2, 27, 29, 46, 52, 69, 94, 102, 103, 104, 105, 107, 110, 116
Thomas Helms, Schwerin 21, 30, 33, 39, 58, 62, 76–79, 89
Herbig-Haarhaus Lackmuseum, Cologne 11
Jürgen Karpinski, Dresden 67
Karin Kiemer, Hamburg 17
Landesbildstelle Bremen 106
Märkisches Museum, Berlin/Lehmann 32, 35, 112, 118
U. H. Mayer, Düsseldorf 3
Museum für Ur- und Frühgeschichte Thüringens, Weimar 31
Museum Viadrina, Frankfurt (Oder)/Huth 115
Nationale Forschungs- und Gedenkstätten Weimar 14, 18, 49
Oberösterreichisches Landesmuseum, Linz/Gangl 20
Joachim Petri, Leipzig 1, 28, 54, 55, 83
Carin Plessing, Leipzig 119
Gerhard Reinhold, Leipzig 40
Rijksmuseum, Amsterdam 34
Savinelli, Milan 99
Hans Scheidulin, Bremen 38, 65, 66
Christa Sembritzki, Leipzig 59, 81
Staatliche Kunsthalle, Karlsruhe 64
Karl Heinz Syring, Flensburg 86, 91
Victoria and Albert Museum, London 42
WAAP, Moscow 84
Karin Wieckhorst, Leipzig 90
Ulrich Windoffer, Leipzig 16
Erika Woldecke, Stralsund 4